The
LIBERTY
Book of
SIMPLE
SEWING

TEXT BY LUCINDA GANDERTON & CHRISTINE LEECH

Photography by Kristin Perers   Illustrations by Lucinda Ganderton

Cincinnati, Ohio

Published by KP Craft, an imprint of F+W Media, Inc.,
10151 Carver Road, Suite 200, Blue Ash OH 45242.
(800) 289-0963.

fw www.fwmedia.com

17 16 15 14 13   5 4 3 2 1

SRN: T1793
ISBN-13: 9781440240980
ISBN-10: 1440240981

Project designs, text, design, layout & illustrations
© 2013 Quadrille Publishing Ltd.
Photography © 2013 Kristin Perers

First published in 2013 by
Quadrille Publishing Ltd.
Alhambra House
27–31 Charing Cross Road
London WC2H 0LS
www.quadrille.co.uk

DISTRIBUTED IN CANADA BY FRASER DIRECT
100 Armstrong Avenue
Georgetown, ON, Canada L7G 5S4
Tel: (905) 877-441

PUBLISHING DIRECTOR Jane O'Shea
COMMISSIONING EDITOR Lisa Pendreigh
EDITOR Alison Wormleighton
ASSISTANT EDITOR Romilly Morgan
PROJECT DESIGNERS Lucinda Ganderton and Christine Leech
CREATIVE DIRECTOR Helen Lewis
ART DIRECTION & DESIGN Claire Peters
DESIGNER Jim Smith
PHOTOGRAPHER Kristin Perers
STYLIST Twig Hutchinson
MODELS Alex Marshall at FM London, Benjamin, Aurelie, and Basil
ILLUSTRATOR Lucinda Ganderton
PRODUCTION DIRECTOR Vincent Smith
PRODUCTION CONTROLLER Sarah Neesam

CONTENTS

INTRODUCTION

Sewing really doesn't need to be complicated. In fact, if you can sew a line of straight stitches then you can make a surprisingly large number of sewn items for your home—curtains, throws, and pillows, for a start. Add curved seams and slipstitching hems into your sewing repertoire and you will have the skills to make the majority of projects in this book, from the largest curtain panel on pages 24–27 to the smallest rag doll on pages 80–87. You don't need to be a skilled seamstress to achieve professional looking results as the projects have all been designed with the novice stitcher in mind, and yet the more experienced maker will undoubtedly find items to spark their sewing imaginations.

Liberty of London has always been a byword for quality, style, and even luxury. Progressive yet traditional, Liberty Art Fabrics are unique in marrying the contemporary with the timeless. This is reflected in The Liberty Book of Simple Sewing, which offers the home sewer a chance to add an element of Liberty style to their interior through the over 25 simple sewing projects. The traditional techniques of hand quilting, for example, are married with the contemporary graphic lines of the chevron on pages 70–75, but also provide the perfect showcase for a range of tonal Liberty Lifestyle craft fabric quilting cottons.

The Liberty Book of Simple Sewing has been created to showcase the variety of Liberty Art Fabrics designed prints, to inspire the reader with their versatility, and to provide an irresistible collection of original designs to create for the home. The range of projects includes core items, such as pillows, as well as more unexpected designs like the graffiti table runner, but they are all characterized by the imaginative use of fabric with often unique combinations of the color and pattern.

Projects such as the no-sew patchwork picture frames on pages 34–37 or the floral garland on pages 88–91 can easily be accomplished in an afternoon, and can even be made from scraps of fabric left over from other projects. At the other end of the spectrum, makes such as the striped throw on pages 144–149 are more labor-intensive investment pieces that are set to become cherished family keepsakes.

ESSENTIAL TOOLS & EQUIPMENT

Notions departments, quilting stores, and online craft stores are full of tempting gadgets, but when assembling your sewing kit bear in mind that you only need a few basic items to make any project in this book. Quality tools, however, are an investment; they will help you achieve a professional result and last for many years. Keep everything organized in a lidded box or make the multi-pocketed sewing tidy on pages 108–113 to keep your equipment at hand.

NEEDLES

There is a special type of needle for each hand sewing task, so start off with a large assorted packet. Needles come in various thicknesses: the larger the number the more slender the needle, and you'll soon find a personal preference. Store them safely in a needlebook or keep them in the packet—they tend to disappear into pincushions.

- "Sharps" are used for most hand stitching and basting. They are medium length and have a small round eye to accommodate a single strand of sewing thread.
- "Betweens" or "quilting" needles are shorter and finer, and slide easily through several layers of fabric.
- "Crewel" needles have long eyes for six-strand cotton embroidery floss. This makes them easy to thread and suitable for all general sewing.

THIMBLES

Thimbles and other finger-guards give vital protection if you are doing a lot of hand stitching and are essential for quilting when you may need one on each hand. If you haven't used one before, it may feel clumsy and ungainly, but do persevere. Steel thimbles come in different sizes, so you should be able to find one that is comfortable, but lightweight silicone thimbles are best of all, molding to fit your fingertip snugly.

PINS

Steel dressmaker's pins are 1–1³/₈" long with tiny heads. They are very fine, so leave no marks in the fabric—ideal for Liberty Tana Lawn. Glass-headed pins, however, are easier to handle and show up well on patterned fabrics. Store your pins in a metal box (with a small magnet) or in a pincushion.

SAFETY PINS

Large safety pins are used for threading ribbon or elastic through casings—you'll need one for the drawstring bag on pages 137–139 or the waistband of the children's pajama pants on pages 118–123. Quilter's safety pins are an invaluable alternative to traditional basting when putting a quilt together. Their curved shape makes them easy to insert through the three layers of fabric and batting.

CUTTING AND SNIPPING

You'll need three different sizes of scissors: each does a very different job.

- Tailor's shears are used for fabric, but never paper which will blunt the long steel blades. The angled handles keep the lower blade flat against the table for precise cutting of large shapes. Look for a pair with comfortable cushioned handles.
- Medium-size household scissors can be used for cutting out smaller fabric items and for all of your paper patterns and templates.
- Small embroidery scissors with a sharp point are ideal for snipping threads, notching seams, and clipping corners.

A round-bladed rotary cutter is always used with a clear plastic quilter's ruler and a self-healing plastic mat. These tools are often used for patchwork, but are also a very quick and accurate means of preparing larger squares and rectangles to given measurements.

MEASURING TOOLS

A long flexible tape measure is essential, and spring-loaded retractable ones are the tidiest. Also, a short plastic ruler is handy for checking hem lengths and seam widths.

MARKING TOOLS

Air-erasable fabric pens are a great innovation: their light-sensitive pigment fades in time, and so they can be used to draw seam allowances, pattern markings, or embroidery outlines on the finest fabrics without leaving any trace of ink. Traditional tailor's chalk shows up on darker and thicker fabrics, and a sharp HB pencil provides a light outline on areas that will be covered.

IRONING

Keep your iron ready for use in your workspace. Iron your fabric well before cutting out and press each seam as you work. A mist spray helps steam out stubborn creases, while fabric stiffener or spray starch gives extra body to fine fabrics.

SECURING AND GLUING

In addition to your sewing kit, you'll need some basic craft equipment. The fabric on the patchwork picture frames on pages 34–37 is glued with a water-soluble liquid adhesive that dries to a clear finish. Double-sided tape is used to secure the fabric cover on the drum lampshade on pages 66–69. The upholstered footstool on pages 140–143 requires a small hammer and decorative nails, and the covered letters on pages 38–43 need a staple gun.

THREAD

Keep a spool of white sewing thread in your sewing box, and a few bright colors for easily identifiable basting. When buying thread for a particular project, you should match the color to the fabric as closely as possible. If you can't find an exact match go for a slightly darker shade. Match fiber to fiber when choosing your thread. Finely spun mercerized cotton thread is best for sewing Liberty Tana Lawn, and poly-cotton works well with heavier Linen Union and Kingly Cord. Use quilting thread for sewing together the layers of throws and quilts.

IRON-ON FUSIBLE BONDING WEB

This heat-sensitive adhesive comes on a paper backing. Use it for tracing, cutting, and bonding appliqué shapes and also to fix two layers of fabric together for projects like the floral garland on pages 88–91 or the pockets on the picnic bag on pages 124–129.

FILLINGS AND STUFFINGS

Furnishing suppliers offer a wide selection of ready-made pillow forms with feather, cotton, or synthetic fillings in standard shapes. Stuff one-off shapes, like the cloud pillows on pages 18–21, with polyester filling fiber, but always check that it meets safety standards before buying. The same applies to toy stuffing—in case of mishaps, this should be washable. Flat cushions, like the chair pads on pages 28–33, have a 1"-thick upholstery foam filling, which can be cut with scissors. Specialty suppliers can cut deeper foam to size.

GETTING STARTED

DRAFTING THE PATTERNS

Many of the projects—including the table mats and leaf pillows—are constructed from simple strips, squares, and rectangles. The dimensions for these are given in the "cutting out" section. To make paper pattern pieces for these shapes, mark the width and depth onto dressmaker's graph paper (large sheets of graph paper with a 1-inch grid) and cut out along the printed lines. Alternatively, use a rotary cutter, a quilter's ruler, and a cutting mat.

Small shaped templates—like those for the Libby doll and her outfit on pages 80–87—are given as half-size outlines that you can photocopy directly from the page, enlarging them at 200%. Larger patterns, such as the children's pajama pants, are shown in a scaled-down version on a square grid. Draw these to full size on dressmaker's graph paper, copying the line within each small square onto its larger equivalent. Copy the markings onto your paper pattern and label each piece clearly.

The size and shape of other projects are variable and will depend on the size of your window or lampshade. Clear guidance is given for measuring up and working out the proportions for these items.

Before you cut out the fabric for any of the projects, always double check that your paper pattern piece is the correct size.

WORKING WITH FABRIC

Look closely at any piece of fabric and you'll see that it's made up of two sets of interwoven threads, which lie at right angles to each other. The long threads that are set onto the loom are known as the warp and they run from top to bottom of the finished cloth, as the "long grain." The threads that are woven between them are called the weft, and run from left to right, as the "side grain." The woven edges are known as the selvages. Always cut these away, as the fabric here is more tightly woven.

Your pattern pieces should always be positioned so that the side edges are parallel to the selvages, and they lie squarely along the "long grain" of the fabric. Pieces that are not cut on the grain can stretch and become distorted.

Many of the Liberty Tana Lawns and Liberty Lifestyle craft fabrics have small-scale motif patterns, so the actual position of the templates isn't critical, but on larger-scale prints they should be placed so that the design lines up on each piece. You'll need to allow extra fabric for this, and also if you are making a set of matching chair pads. Center large motifs, and if you are working with stripes or ginghams, make sure you cut the pieces parallel with the lines.

CUTTING OUT
Press your material to get rid of any creases before you pin on the pattern pieces, then smooth it out flat on your work surface. The double-ended arrow on the pattern indicates the direction of the grain and this should always point from top to bottom of the fabric. Cut out around the outside edges of the pattern with your shears, keeping the angled handle downward and making smooth strokes.

KNOW YOUR SEWING MACHINE
You may be an experienced stitcher with a trusted workhorse of a machine, but for the new enthusiast the variety of machines in a department store can be confusing. These range from simple plastic entry-level versions to high-tech computerized models. Go to a reputable dealer, try them all out, and spend time talking to the knowledgeable sales team—but don't be tempted to overspend. Study the manual carefully—it tells you all the technical information and will have a useful trouble-shooting section.

All that's needed for simple sewing projects is a reliable machine with a few basic functions: the ability to cope with thicker fabrics, a zigzag stitch for finishing raw edges, and a regular straight stitch with an even tension. Use the basic foot for everything except sewing in zippers—you won't need the buttonhole foot or the more specialized dressmaking feet for the straightforward sewing in this book.

Some machines will automatically adjust the presser foot when sewing different weight fabrics, but on others you have to change a lever. Don't forget to do this, as a fine fabric like Liberty Tana Lawn needs less pressure than Liberty Linen Union. Always match the gauge of the needle to the material being sewn: fine for lawn cotton and a thicker one for canvas or heavy calico. Change the needles regularly, as a blunt or snagged point creates irregular stitches. And if your machine doesn't come with a hard case, you can always stitch your own cover using the instructions on pages 134–137.

HEMS AND BINDING

There are two ways to finish an exposed edge: by turning it under and stitching down the fold to make a hem or by binding it with a narrow strip of fabric.

SINGLE HEM
Finish the raw edge of the fabric with a zigzag or overlock stitch. With the right side face down, fold the edge to the wrong side to the given depth, pressing it with a hot iron as you proceed. Use a ruler to keep this measurement constant. Pin the hem in place, then machine stitch just below the zigzag, or stitch by hand.

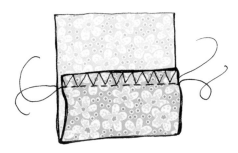

DOUBLE HEM
This more durable finish is made up of two turnings and is used for curtains and garments. Fold and press the first turning as above, then measure and press a second turning to conceal the raw edge. Pin and baste, then slipstitch by hand or machine stitch $1/8$" from the inner fold.

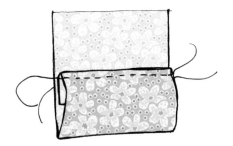

BOUND EDGE

To bind the edges of a quilt you can use ready-made bias binding (which you can buy in a range of Liberty prints) or make your own straight binding from matching or contrasting fabric. Cut a long, narrow strip four times the finished depth. Press it in half, then press the raw edges to the center crease and unfold.

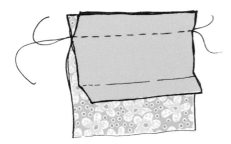

Pin the binding along the edge of the quilt with the right sides facing and raw edges matching. Machine stitch along the first crease line.

Refold the bottom crease, turn the binding over to the back and baste in place. Slipstitch along the fold or machine stitch just inside the edge of the binding. To bind a curved edge, like those on the cafetière cover on pages 62–65 you will need to use ready-made bias binding and stretch it gently to fit around the curved corners.

SEAMS AND JOINS

Before two pieces of fabric are seamed together they have to be joined temporarily with pins and/or basting. Hold them with right sides together and align the raw edges. Insert a pin at each corner, then along the rest of the edge. You can position the pins parallel to the edge, or if you are not going to baste the seam, put them in at right angles, so that they can easily be pulled out as the fabric passes under the presser foot. A line of basting—long running stitches—makes a stable foundation for machine stitching. Sew just inside the seam line with a contrasting thread that will be removed when the seam is complete.

The width of the seam allowance—the spare fabric that lies within a seam—is specified for each individual project. For Liberty Tana Lawn or Liberty Lifestyle craft fabric, it's usually $3/8$", or $5/8$" for heavier fabrics. Like all patchwork, the chevron quilt blocks are joined with a narrow $1/4$" seam. To keep this width consistent, line the raw edges up against the corresponding parallel line, which you'll find etched onto the sewing machine's base plate. Hold the fabric in this position as you guide it under the presser foot.

Press each seam as it is completed to give your work a crisp finish. Sometimes the seam allowance is pressed to one side, but where a flat finish is required the seam is pressed open. Do this by gently parting the two sides of the allowance with the tip of the iron.

STRAIGHT SEAM

With right sides together, machine stitch the two edges with the given seam allowance. It's always a good idea to reinforce both ends of the seam with a few reverse stitches so that the ends don't come undone. Press the seam allowance open or to one side as directed.

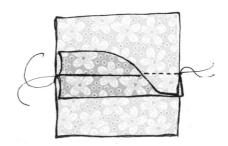

FRENCH SEAM

This enclosed seam gives a neat look on both back and front, and is used to make the curtain panel on pages 24–27. Pin the two edges with wrong sides together and stitch with a 1/4" seam. Now trim the seam allowance to 1/8" and refold the fabric so that the right sides are together and the raw edges lie inside. For accuracy, you can baste the front and back together, making sure the seam lies along the edge. Stitch the seam again, taking the required allowance, then press the seam to one side.

OVERLOCKED SEAM

Garment seams are finished on the inside to prevent them from fraying when washed. After stitching a straight seam, trim the seam allowance as necessary, then machine zigzag or overlock stitch the two edges together before pressing.

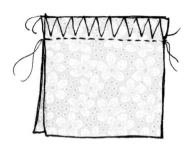

TOPSTITCHED SEAM

Topstitching reinforces a seam and gives a neat finish. After stitching a straight seam, press the seam allowance to one side then sew through all three layers on the right side, 1/8" from the seam line, using the inside space on the presser foot as a guide.

OUTSIDE CURVED SEAM

This technique is used for the edged pillowcase on pages 102–107 and the cloud pillows and mobile on pages 18–23. Start by trimming the seam allowance to 1/4".

Around an outside curve, cut out a series of tiny triangles to within 1/8" of the stitching line to reduce the bulk. This enables the seam to lie flat when it is turned right side out and pressed.

CORNER SEAM

Stitch along the seam allowance as far as the corner. Keeping the needle down, raise the presser foot. Pivot the fabric, then continue along the next edge. Reduce the bulk by trimming away a triangle of surplus fabric at the corner. Turn right side out and gently ease out the point with a knitting needle or a pencil.

INSIDE CURVED SEAM

Make a row of little snips into the seam allowance along an inside curve. (Cut right into the space between two adjacent curves.) Use this technique for the edged pillowcase on pages 102–107 and the cloud pillows and mobile on pages 18–23.

REINFORCING STITCHES

Straps and handles, such as the dog lead on pages 48–49 for instance, need to be stitched down in a way that gives them extra strength. Press under $\frac{3}{8}$" and baste in place. Starting at the bottom left corner, machine stitch a rectangle across the end, then stitch up to the top right corner, across to the top left corner, down to bottom right and back to the start point. You may find it helpful to mark the outline first.

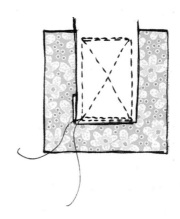

HAND STITCHING

HAND STITCHES
Careful preparation and hand finishing give a professional finish to any needlework project, so here are the four basic stitches that you will need to seam, gather, baste, add trimmings, and close openings.

RUNNING STITCH
This simple stitch is used for joining, gathering, and quilting. The spaces and stitches are equal and the length is between $\frac{1}{8}$" and $\frac{1}{4}$" depending on the thickness of the cloth. With practice, and using a long needle, you should be able to pick up two or three stitches at a time. Make longer stitches when basting, or use the dressmaker's variation below. A line of running stitch is used for gathering by hand and the thread is pulled up to create a ruffle.

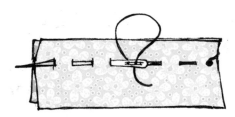

DRESSMAKER'S BASTING
A temporary line of basting holds two pieces of fabric together before they are sewn by machine. The length of the individual stitches doesn't really matter as long as the seam is aligned accurately, but generally they should be about $\frac{3}{4}$" for thick fabrics and $\frac{3}{8}$" for finer materials. The stitches are about twice as long as the spaces between them.

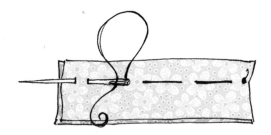

OVERCAST STITCH
Use this stitch for sewing on braids, such as the bobble fringing that embellishes the chair pads. Work a line of short diagonal stitches over the edge of the trimming, in a matching thread.

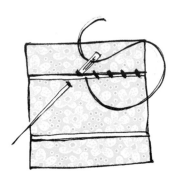

SLIPSTITCH
This joining stitch produces a flat, unobtrusive seam. It's used to hold together two folded edges on either side of an opening, like that on the cloud pillows.

Bring the needle out through the bottom fold and, keeping it roughly horizontal, insert the point through the top fold, directly above the start point. Push the tip through the top fold so that it emerges $\frac{1}{4}$" farther along, then pull the needle through. Insert it directly below and repeat the same action to the end of the seam.

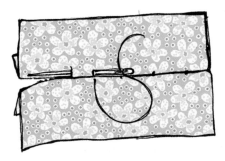

Slipstitch can also be used to attach a folded edge to a flat, single layer. Bring the needle out through the folded edge and insert it into the single, flat layer directly above. Make a stitch picking up only about three threads, then push the needle through the folded edge so it emerges $\frac{1}{4}$" farther along. Repeat.

PATCHWORK & APPLIQUÉ

A patchwork quilt consists of three layers: the pieced top which is made up from individual patches, the batting that gives it warmth and thickness, and the plain backing fabric.

The pieces for the chevron quilt are quickly and easily cut on a self-healing mat, with a standard 6-inch quilter's square and a sharp rotary cutter. Replace the blades regularly, as they dull with use or can become nicked. Patchwork is traditionally stitched with a $1/4$" seam. This distance is marked on most machines, or you can buy a specially designed narrow foot to keep a regular seam.

There are several types of batting for the center layer of the quilt sandwich. Thick polyester is tactile and puffy, and easy to wash and dry for everyday use. Natural cotton and bamboo fibers are lighter and give a soft, draped look to the finished quilt. They will shrink slightly when laundered and the slightly puckered effect that this produces gives depth and texture to the quilt.

You can join two lengths of fabric for the back of your quilt, but "whole cloth," or a single width, saves time. Look for an old bed sheet in good condition, or buy new sheet fabric or extra-wide fabric in a color to complement the quilt top.

QUILTING

Once you have assembled the three layers (the project step-by-step instructions tell you just how to do this) it's time to hand quilt. Use tightly spun quilting thread for this and a short, slender needle. Quilting stitch is simply a small, regular running stitch, which is worked either "in the ditch"— along the seam line between patches—or $1/8$"–$1/4$" outside the seam, as an outline. You'll find your own preferred way of working after a while, with one hand above and one below the quilt. Roll up the area not being used and place it either on the table in front of you, or over your lap to keep you cozy in the colder months.

Start each length of thread invisibly in the traditional way. Make a tiny knot at one end and insert the needle at the start point. Gently pull the thread and you'll feel the knot "pop" through the fabric. Work a backstitch to secure it, then sew along the quilting line. Finish off with three tiny stitches on top of each other and take the needle through the batting. Bring it up $1/4$" away and clip the end close to the surface. With a bit of wiggling about it will disappear neatly into the quilt.

Small projects like the cafetière cover can be machine quilted with closely spaced parallel lines. Make sure that the layers are basted or pinned together well before machine stitching or they will slide around. Larger quilted items need a special "walking foot," which minimizes the risk of movement.

APPLIQUÉ

IRON-ON FUSIBLE BONDING WEB

This invaluable aid to appliqué is a heat-sensitive adhesive mounted on paper. It melts under the heat of an iron to fuse two layers of fabric together and comes in heavy- and light-bond weights. Choose a heavy bond for thicker fabrics and light bond for Tana Lawn, such as on the leaf pillows on pages 96–101.

Bearing in mind that the motif has to be reversed, trace the outline onto the paper side of the bonding web and cut the shape out roughly. Following the manufacturer's instructions, press the adhesive onto the appliqué fabric to fuse it in place, then cut out around the pencil line. Peel off the backing paper, position the motif—the right way up—on the backing fabric, and press down. Use an up-and-down action rather than a sliding motion to prevent any distortion of the appliqué motif. Finish the raw edges with a narrow machine satin stitch in a matching or contrasting color thread. Some machines have a blanket or feather stitch function, which will give a more decorative look.

PROJECTS

CLOUD PILLOWS

All you need is one yard or less of medium-weight cotton fabric in your favorite print to make a cute cumulus-shaped pillow.

YOU WILL NEED

for the large pillow
- 28" x 36" of Liberty Lifestyle craft fabric in print of your choice (we used Garnett in colorway C)

for the medium-size pillow
- 44" x 14" of Liberty Lifestyle craft fabric in print of your choice (we used Woolf in colorway C)

for the small pillow
- 40" x 12" of Liberty Lifestyle craft fabric in print of your choice (we used in Catherine colorway C)

for all pillow sizes
- matching sewing thread
- 17 ½ ounces of safety-standard polyester pillow filling
- sewing machine
- sewing kit

TEMPLATE

Copy the template on page 151, enlarging it by 250%, 325%, or 400%, depending on the pillow size.

CUTTING OUT

from Liberty Lifestyle craft fabric print
two clouds in your chosen size (one reversed)

The large, medium-size, and small pillows are made in the same way, regardless of size.

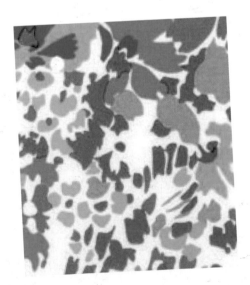

GARNETT *is based on several 1930s Liberty designs. It was first printed at Liberty's Merton Abbey Print Works on wool in 1971.*

18

❶ PINNING THE COVER TOGETHER

Place the two clouds with the right sides together. Align the curves and pin around the outside edge, leaving a 6" opening along the bottom edge.

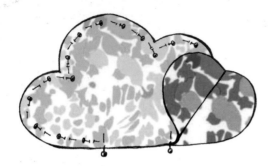

❷ SEWING AND TRIMMING THE SEAM

Sew the pillow pieces together with a ⅝" seam. To maintain a consistent seam width, line the edge of the fabric up with the ⅝" mark on the throat plate as you sew. Start at the left edge of the opening and reinforce both ends of the seam with a few reverse stitches. Trim the seam allowance to ⅜" all around.

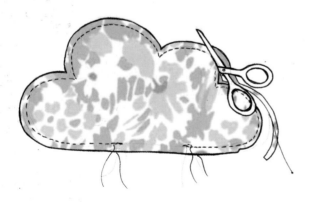

❸ NOTCHING THE SEAM ALLOWANCE

Now cut out a series of small notches around each curve to create a smooth outline. Cut to within ⅛" of the stitching and space the notches about 1½" apart; closer together on the tighter curves. Snip a deep V-shape at the inward points where the curves meet.

❹ TURNING THE COVER RIGHT SIDE OUT

Press back the ⅜" seam allowance along the bottom edge, then turn the cover right side out through the opening. Ease out the curved seams, then press the cover, pulling gently on the inward points to allow the fabric to stretch.

❺ FILLING THE PILLOW WITH STUFFING

Fill the cover with the polyester pillow filling. Keep a continuous stream of stuffing going into the pillow and push it right up into each curve; do not break the stuffing off in clumps as this can make the pillow lumpy.

❻ SEWING UP THE OPENING

Pin the two sides of the opening together. Using small neat slipstitches, hand sew it closed. Mold the finished pillow with your hands to distribute the filling evenly within the cover. Pass a warm iron over the curves to remove any remaining creases.

CLOUD MOBILE

After sewing the cloud pillows,
you'll find yourself left with some
corner scraps of spare fabric, which are
perfect for making this mobile.

YOU WILL NEED

- 24" x 8" of turquoise cotton fabric
- 20" x 6" of Liberty Lifestyle craft fabric in three prints of your choice (we used the corner remnants left over from making the Cloud Pillows—Catherine in colorway C, Garnet in colorway C, and Woolf in colorway C)
- 28 assorted clear and blue glass drop beads
- 28 round $1/8$" silver glass beads
- safety-standard polyester pillow or toy filling
- matching sewing thread
- silver sewing thread
- silver ring, for hanging
- sewing machine
- sewing kit

TEMPLATE

Copy the template on page 151, enlarging it by 130% for the small cloud and 160% for the large cloud.

CUTTING OUT

from turquoise cotton fabric
two large clouds (one reversed)

from each of three prints
two small clouds (one reversed)

❶ MAKING THE CLOUDS

These tiny clouds are made in the same way as the Cloud Pillows, so refer to the detailed instructions on page 20. Pin and baste the two pieces with right sides together, and stitch with a $3/8$" seam, leaving a $2\frac{1}{2}$" opening along the bottom edge.

2 Trim the seam allowance back to ¼" and notch the curves. Press back the bottom seam allowance, turn right side out, and ease out the seams. Press lightly, stuff with polyester filling, and slipstitch the opening closed.

3 ADDING THE RAINDROPS

Sew seven glass drops at ¾"–1¼" intervals along the bottom edge of each small cloud. Thread a fine needle with silver sewing thread and secure the end to the seam line. Add a small round bead, then a glass drop. Take the needle back up through the round bead and re-insert at the start point. Pull up the thread until the strand is 2"–3¼" long.

4 Secure the strand with two small stitches, then pass the needle back through the cloud and out again ¾"–1¼" farther along the seam line, ready for the next bead. Hang the largest bead at the center.

5 GETTING THE RIGHT BALANCE

Fasten a 16" length of silver sewing thread to the top of each cloud, centered between the two large dots marked on the template. Make a hanging loop for the large cloud by passing the thread through the metal ring and sewing it back onto the cloud.

6 Pin the small clouds along the bottom edge of the large cloud. Pull up the center cloud so the thread is about 3¼" long and the other two measure approximately 8" and 10". Wrap the ends of the thread around pins to keep them at the right length, then hang up the mobile. Adjust the length of the threads (and possibly their positions) until all four clouds hang straight: this step involves a bit of trial and error. Secure the threads in their final positions.

7 FINISHING OFF

Add the remaining beads to the bottom edge of the large cloud, spacing them evening between the hanging threads.

CURTAIN PANEL

Use the full widths of both the linen fabric and your chosen Liberty print to make this delightfully floaty curtain, which filters light and provides privacy.

YOU WILL NEED

- 53" x 32" of plain fine linen fabric
- 53" x 22" of Liberty Tana Lawn in print of your choice (we used Marina Seaflower in colorway D)
- matching sewing thread
- sewing machine
- sewing kit
- expanding café curtain pole to fit inside your window frame

MEASURING UP
Finished width = 53"
Finished drop = half the height of the window

Our curtain is approximately 38" long: reduce the depth of the main panel to make a shorter curtain and reduce the width of each piece to make a narrower curtain.

CUTTING OUT
Label each piece as you cut it out, so the pieces don't get mixed up.

from plain fine linen fabric
main panel	one 53"-x-25½" rectangle
strip 2	one 53"-x-3¼" strip
strip 4	one 53"-x-2¾" strip

from Liberty Tana Lawn print
strip 1	one 53"-x-5" strip
strip 3	one 53"-x-4" strip
strip 5	one 53"-x-3¼" strip
binding	two 1½"-wide strips, each length of finished depth + ¾"
casing	one 53"-x-2¾" strip
	one 2½"-x-2¾" rectangle

❶ HEMMING THE FIRST FABRIC-PRINT STRIP

Press under 3/8" along the bottom edge of strip 1.
Press under 3/8" once again to make a double hem.
Pin the hem and machine stitch it 1/8" from the
inner fold.

❷ JOINING ON A LINEN STRIP

The strips are all joined with French seams, which
enclose the raw edges and give a neat finish on both
sides of the curtain. Pin strip 2 to strip 1 with wrong
sides together and machine stitch 1/4" from the edge.
Trim the seam allowance to 1/8". Press the seam open.

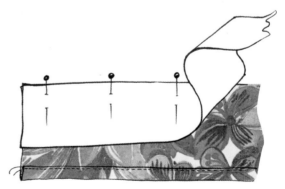

26

❸ COMPLETING THE FRENCH SEAM

Fold the right sides together along the seam line and press. Baste the layers together and machine stitch ³/₈" from the fold.

❻

Press back the overlap in line with the hem. Turn the binding to the wrong side of the curtain and pin so that the folded edge lies just inside the stitching line. Slipstitch the fold in place, taking care not to let the stitches show on the right side.

❹ ADDING THE OTHER STRIPS

Join on strips 3, 4, and 5 in the same way, then sew the top edge of strip 5 to the bottom edge of the main panel. Press each seam so that the allowances lie over the fabric print.

❺ BINDING THE EDGES

Press under ¹/₄" along one long edge of each binding strip. With right sides together, pin the raw edge of one strip to one side edge of the curtain, leaving a ³/₈" overlap at the bottom corner. Machine stitch in place, leaving a ¹/₄" seam allowance.

❼ MAKING THE CASING

With right sides together, pin and stitch the extra piece to the casing strip, with a ¹/₄" seam. Press the seam open. Press and machine stitch a narrow double hem at each short edge, adjusting the length to match the curtain width. Press under ¹/₄" along one long edge of the casing. With right sides together, pin and stitch the raw edge to the top edge of the curtain. Finish as for the side bindings. Slot the pole through the casing and adjust to fit inside the window frame.

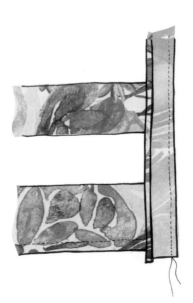

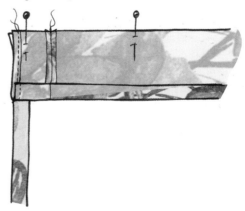

CHAIR PADS

Enliven plain metal or wooden kitchen chairs with made-to-measure seat pads, which provide color as well as comfort.

YOU WILL NEED

for each chair pad
- approximately 24" square of Liberty Linen Union in print of your choice (we used Hebe in colorway A)
- approximately 24" square of plain furnishing-weight fabric in contrasting or matching color, for the backing
- approximately 20" square of 1"-thick safety-standard cushion foam
- approximately 1³/4 yd of bobble edging in contrasting color
- 18" of self-adhesive magnetic strip for metal chairs or 1¹/2 yd of woven cotton tape for wooden chairs

- permanent marker pen
- air-erasable fabric pen or chalk pencil
- large sheet of cardboard (if fabric has a large-scale pattern)
- matching sewing thread
- sheet of newspaper
- sewing machine
- sewing kit

NOTE

If you are using a fabric with a large repeat pattern, like the one shown here, you will need to allow extra length if all your pads are to be identical. To calculate more exact fabric amounts, make your paper templates before purchasing your fabric.

HEBE *is a one-color version of Liberty's famous peacock feather pattern. This design has been in the range since the 1890s and is one of the key prints associated with Liberty.*

❶ MAKING THE TEMPLATES

Cut a sheet of newspaper roughly to the size of your chair seat, tape it to your chair and draw around the outside edge of the seat. Cut along this line. To make the template symmetrical, fold the newspaper in half vertically and trim both edges. This process may take a bit of trial and error, but you will end up with a perfect fit. If you want your pillow to have ties, mark the position of the two outer chair-back struts on the template.

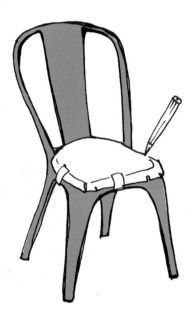

❷ Place the paper template centrally on the sheet of card, draw around the edge and neatly cut out to create a window template. You can now line up this frame on your fabric to select the area of pattern. If your print does not have a large-scale pattern repeat, omit this step and simply use the newspaper template.

❸ CUTTING OUT THE CHAIR PAD TOP

Position the window template on the wrong side of the print fabric and move it around to find an interesting, symmetrical section of the pattern. Draw around the inside of the template, using a chalk pencil for a dark fabric or an air-erasable fabric marker for a light fabric.

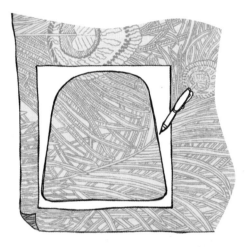

❹ ADDING THE ALLOWANCES

To allow for the thickness of the foam, add on an extra ³⁄₈" all around plus a ³⁄₈" seam allowance. Using a clear ruler or quilter's square as a guide, draw a line ³⁄₄" outside your marked outline. Cut neatly around this line.

❺ SEWING THE COVER TOP TO THE BACKING

Pin the chair pad top to the backing fabric, with right sides together, leaving a 6" opening at the top edge. If you are adding ties, cut the cotton tape in half and then fold each length in half. Referring back to the template, pin the folds to the edge of the chair pad top, in line with the strut marks. Baste the pieces together, then machine stitch ³⁄₈" from the edge, leaving the 6" opening unstitched. Reinforce both ends of the seam with a few reverse stitches. Trim the backing fabric in line with the chair pad top.

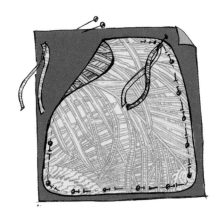

❻ NOTCHING THE CORNERS

For perfectly smooth curves at the corners, you will need to notch the seam allowance. Cut a series of small triangles from the seam allowance to within ¹⁄₈" of the stitching, spacing them approximately ³⁄₄" apart.

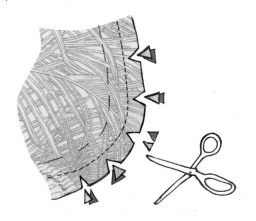

❼ TURNING THE COVER RIGHT SIDE OUT

Press back the seam allowance along either side of the opening, then turn the cover right side out. Ease out the seams and lightly press. The ties, if you have added them, will now be on the right side.

❽ CUTTING OUT THE FOAM

Using a permanent marker, draw around the template onto the foam; cut out the foam. Roll it roughly into thirds and insert through the opening in the cover. As the cover is designed to fit tightly, you will need to manipulate the foam until it sits flat. Work around the edge of the chair pad to center the seam line.

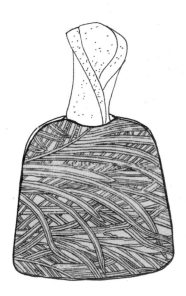

❾ ADDING THE MAGNETIC STRIPS

If you are placing the pillows on metal chairs, use self-adhesive magnetic strips to anchor the pads to the chair. Slip one 4" length along each side of the foam, with the adhesive side facing the foam, and press into place.

❿ ADDING THE FINISHING TOUCHES

Pin the two sides of the opening together and hand stitch it closed. Starting at the center back, pin and then overcast stitch the bobble edging in place all the way around the cushion seam line.

PATCHWORK PICTURE FRAMES

With these print-covered picture frames
you can create a stunning effect with
fabric without even sewing a stitch.

YOU WILL NEED

for the patchwork frame
- selection of scraps of Liberty Tana Lawn in prints of your choice (for the green frame, we used Speckle in colorway C, May Rose in colorway A, and Xanthe Sunbeam in colorway C; and for the purple frame, we used Ottilia in colorway C, Pointillism in colorway A, and Tresco in colorway D)

for the plain frame
- rectangle of Liberty Tana Lawn 3¼" larger all around than your frame in print of your choice (we used Pointillism in colorway A)

for both style plain frames
- old picture frames
- scissors
- clear-drying white craft glue
- sandpaper or sanding block
- old paintbrush
- stencil brush

PREPARING THE FRAME

To ensure the fabric properly adheres to the existing finish, key the surface by sanding the whole frame. A sanding block is especially good for sanding intricate moldings.

TRESCO *is a watercolor study of a selection of flowers, ferns, and succulents from the Tresco Abbey Garden in the Isles of Scilly.*

covering a frame in patchwork pieces

❶ WORKING OUT THE DESIGN

Cut out a selection of rectangles from the various fabric prints, each one wide enough to wrap right around the frame with an overlap at each edge. Lay them out over the frame to work out the best arrangement. When you are happy with the design, lift them off one by one and lay them out in the same order on your work surface.

❷ STICKING DOWN THE FABRIC PIECES

Paint the area of the frame that corresponds to the first fabric piece with a thin coat of glue, making sure you cover the top and side edges. If your frame is very ornate, make sure you get glue into all the nooks and crannies. While the glue is still tacky place the fabric, right side up, over the glue-coated area and gently press it down.

❸ To get the fabric to sit right into the frame, use a clean stencil brush to press it down with a dabbing action.

❹ Now turn the frame over, coat the back with glue and stick down the fabric. Continue adding fabric pieces until you reach the corners. Fold under and stick down a narrow turning along the overlapping edge of each new fabric piece to produce a neat join.

❺ COVERING THE CORNERS

Glue the top and sides of the corner area, lay the fabric in place and smooth down the top. Fold the outside corner downward to check the height of the frame, then cut off a small triangle just outside this point. Snip into the inside corner, right up to the frame. Smooth down the sides.

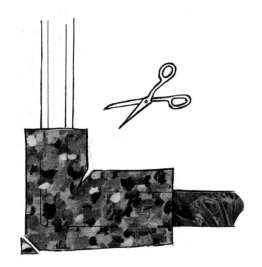

❻ NEATENING THE BACK

Paint the reverse of the frame with glue and, stretching the fabric slightly, fold the inside margins to the back. Fold over the margin at the outside corner, then the outside edges. When the glue is dry you can cover up any gaps on the inside corners with small pieces of fabric.

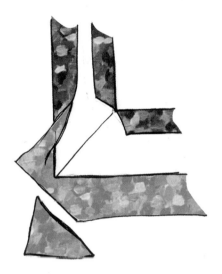

covering a frame in a single fabric

❶ Place the fabric on a flat surface, right side up, and lay the frame on top. Cut away the fabric from the center of the frame, leaving a wide enough margin to cover the sides and wrap around to the back. Snip into the corners as before.

❷ Coat the whole frame with a layer of glue, diluting it very slightly if it starts to dry out too quickly. Lay the fabric right side up over the frame. Press it down with a stencil brush and finish off as for the patchwork frame.

COVERED LETTERS

This simple but effective no-sew project involves manipulating fabric over readily available decoupage bases. So now whatever you want to say, you can spell it in Liberty print.

YOU WILL NEED

- Liberty Tana Lawn in print of your choice (see note; we used Pinky in colorway A, Saeed in colorway B, Hugo Grenville in colorway D, and Tresco in colorway A)
- fleece fabric or thin batting (see tip)
- wooden or particleboard letter, ³/₈" thick
- sheet of medium-weight cardboard, the same size as the letter
- ¹/₂"-wide double-sided tape
- staple gun
- glue stick
- scissors

NOTE

Choose a Liberty Tana Lawn with a small-scale, busy pattern so that any areas where you have to layer the fabric will be less noticeable.

TIP

A base layer of fleece fabric or thin batting gives a softly padded look to the finished letter.

CUTTING OUT

If your letter is thicker than ³/₈", allow more fabric for the coverings.

from Liberty Tana Lawn print

front covering   one rectangle, 1¹/₂" larger all around than the letter

back covering   one rectangle, ³/₄" larger all around than the letter

from fleece fabric or thin batting

padding   one rectangle, 1¹/₂" larger all around than the letter

PINKY *was painted by five-year-old pupils from St Bartholomew's School, London.*

❶ PREPARING THE CARDBOARD BACKING

Draw around the letter onto the cardboard and cut out around the outline. This will be used to neaten the back of the letter later on.

❷ CUTTING THE FLEECE TO SIZE

Stick double-sided tape around the back edges of the letter, cutting short lengths to fit around any curves. Peel off the backing papers and place the letter face down onto the padding. Trim the padding so that there is a 1¼" margin all around the letter.

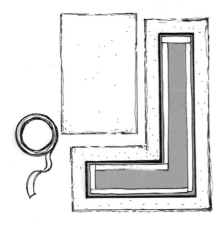

❸ Clip off the surplus padding at each corner, snipping to within ⅛" of the letter and cutting at a 45-degree angle. Cut into the margin at the inside angles so the padding will wrap neatly around the letter.

❹ TURNING BACK THE MARGINS

Starting at the center of a long edge and working outward toward the corners, gently pull the edge of the padding onto the tape and press it down. Fold over the short end, then continue around the letter until all the margins are turned back.

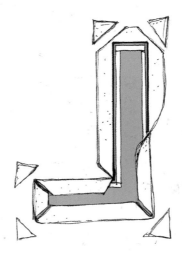

❺ COVERING THE LETTER WITH FABRIC

Place the letter, face down in the center of the front fabric covering. Trim the margin to 1¼" all around. Fold back the fabric margins and staple them down, starting in the center of a straight edge and working toward the corners to keep the fabric smooth.

⑥ FITTING FABRIC AROUND CURVES

To cover an outside curve, pleat the fabric slightly and pull it toward the center of the letter. Position the staples close together. For an inner curve, cover the entire edge with a matching fabric strip. Clip into the margin of the front covering at right angles, spacing the cuts at ⅝" intervals and snipping to within ⅛" of the letter. Coat the back of the fabric with glue and stick down over the matching fabric strip.

⑦ MITERING THE CORNERS

When you get to a corner, miter the surplus fabric for a neat finish. Turn the corner back at an angle, stretching it gently for a neat edge, and staple down the point. Fold over the margin along the next side of the letter and continue stapling.

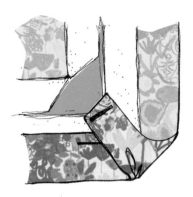

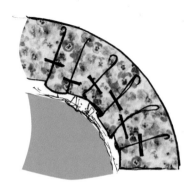

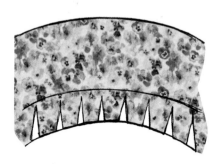

❽ DEALING WITH INSIDE ANGLES

You will need to add an extra layer of fabric at each inside angle, or the letter will peep through the cover. Cut a 1½" strip, the same depth as the letter and fix it across the corner with double-sided tape. Snip into the margin at 45 degrees, run a glue stick over reverse side to hold it tightly in place, then staple as before.

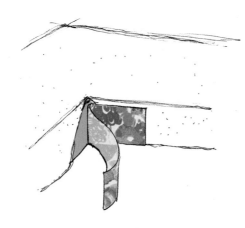

❾ COVERING LETTERS WITH HOLES

Cover the inside edge of the corners or curves with fabric strips to conceal the padding. Cut it deeper than the thickness of the letter, so it overlaps the back by ³⁄₈". Cover the entire letter with fabric as above, then snip at intervals into the taut fabric across the hole, cutting from the center outward. Make a row of cuts along a curve, as in step 6, or snip into any angles as for step 8. Coat the back of the fabric with a glue stick and wrap each section around the fabric-covered edge to the back.

❿ MAKING THE BACK

Stick lengths of double-sided tape along each edge of the cardboard letter. Lay out the back fabric covering with the right side face down and position the cardboard letter on top, right side up. Trim the fabric so that there is a ⁵⁄₈" margin all around the edges of the letter. Trim off the surplus fabric across each corner, cutting to within ¹⁄₈" of the cardboard and snip into the margins along any curves and inside angles. Peel the protective backing paper from the double-sided tape, then fold back the fabric margins and press them onto the adhesive strips.

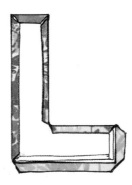

⓫ Cover the entire back with a layer of double-sided tape. Take off the backing paper and press it firmly in place onto the reverse of the wooden letter.

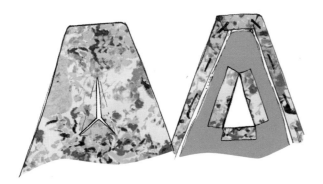

43

FABRIC BELT

*Customize an otherwise plain raincoat
or other coat with a Liberty print belt and
covered buttons (see page 47); a simple
way to update an outfit each season.*

YOU WILL NEED

- 44" x 8" of Liberty Lifestyle craft fabric in print of your choice (we used Newbury in colorway A)
- 36" x 8" of medium-weight black cotton fabric, for the backing
- air-erasable fabric pen or sharp pencil
- black sewing thread
- large safety pin
- belt buckle (without a prong) to fit 2½" belt

❶ PREPARING THE FABRIC STRIPS

Cut out two 3¼"-wide strips from the fabric print, one 43½" long and the other 25½" long, carefully matching the repeat. Sew them together as in step 1 of the dog leash on page 48 so that you have a 68¼"-long strip. Cut and join the black fabric so that you have a 3¼"-x-68¼" backing strip.

❷ MARKING THE CURVED END

Using a saucer or small plate as your guide, mark a curved line across one end of the main fabric strip. Draw onto the wrong side of the fabric with an air-erasable fabric pen or sharp pencil.

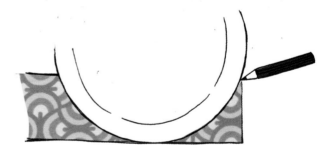

NEWBURY *is based on a 1965 design by Agnes Roberts for Liberty. It was printed at Liberty's Merton Abbey Print Works on cotton in 1966.*

❸ SEWING THE TWO HALVES TOGETHER

Pin the two sides of the belt with the right sides together. Starting at the center of one long edge, machine stitch all the way around, ³/₈" from the edge. Follow the curved line carefully to round off the corner and finish the stitching line 4" from the starting point. Press back the ³/₈" seam allowance on each side of the opening.

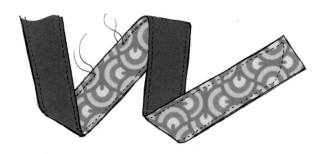

❹ TRIMMING THE SEAM ALLOWANCE

Trim the seam allowance along the curve to ¹/₄". Snip a sharply angled triangle from each side of the point, then snip a series of little triangles along the curve. Cut to within ¹/₈" of the seam line and space them about ¹/₄" apart. Clip a shallow arrowhead shape from the two corners at the other end.

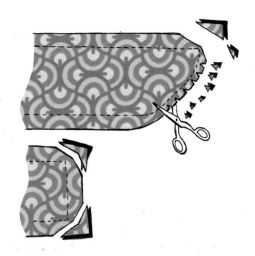

❺ TURNING RIGHT SIDE OUT

Fix a large safety pin to one end of the belt. Gently feed it between the two layers of fabric toward the center and out of the opening. Do the same at the other end, then ease out the seams and shape the corners with the point of a pencil. Press the edges lightly.

❻ TOPSTITCHING THE EDGE

Baste the two sides of the opening together. Using black thread, machine stitch all the way around the belt, ¹/₈" from the edge.

❼ SEWING ON THE BUCKLE

Slide the buckle onto the straight end of the belt, then fold under 2" and baste. Sew in place with two lines of machine stitching, ¹/₄" from the end.

COVERED BUTTONS

Covering buttons is a useful technique for anyone to have in their sewing repertoire, as it's a speedy yet impactful way to customize any garment.

YOU WILL NEED

- self-cover buttons—the same size and number as on your coat or garment
- Liberty Lifestyle craft fabric in print of your choice (we used Newbury in colorway A)—allow approximately 4" x 4" for each button, depending on the scale of the motifs
- tracing paper
- air-erasable fabric pen
- matching sewing thread
- sewing kit

CUTTING OUT

Cut out a circle of tracing paper ⅝" larger all around than your button; or cut around the printed circle on the button packaging, and use the circle void as a window template. Lay the fabric right side up and center the template over a pleasing part of the design. Draw around the template with an air-erasable fabric pen and cut out the fabric circle around the outline. For a matching set, use the same pattern area for each button.

❶ GATHERING THE FABRIC

Using a double length of thread, sew a line of small running stitches around the fabric circle, ¼" from the edge. Leave long tails at the beginning and end to make the gathering easier.

❷ INSERTING THE BUTTON FRONT

Pull the two tails until the fabric is loosely gathered, then insert the button front. Pull the threads up tightly. Check that the fabric pattern is still centered and that the button loop is horizontal, then knot the threads securely. Trim the ends.

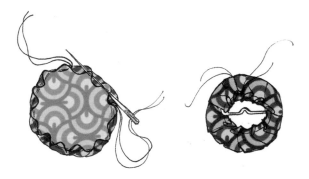

❸ SNAPPING ON THE BACK

Check that the gathers are evenly distributed, then press the button back firmly in place to enclose the raw edges.

DOG LEASH

With a small amount of Liberty print fabric and by sewing just a few straight seams, you ensure that you and your faithful canine companion are fully coordinated with matching dog leash, belt, and buttons.

YOU WILL NEED

- 44" x 6" of Liberty Lifestyle craft fabric in print of your choice for the main fabric (we used Newbury in colorway A), —if you need to pattern match a larger-scale print, allow more depth
- 44" x 5" of medium-weight black cotton fabric, for the backing
- ³/₄"-wide iron-on fusible hem tape
- metal dog leash clip
- black sewing thread
- sewing machine
- sewing kit

CALCULATING THE STRIP LENGTH
To calculate the length of the main-fabric and backing strips, measure your dog's existing leash from end to end, then add another 10³/₄" for the handle loop and clip turn-back.

❶ PREPARING THE FABRIC STRIPS

Cut the main fabric into two matching 1³/₄"-x-44" strips. With right sides together, stitch the ends together with a ³/₈" seam, lining up the repeat if possible. Press the seam open. Trim the strip to the right length for your dog's leash. Cut two 2"-x-44" strips from the backing fabric, then join and trim them in the same way.

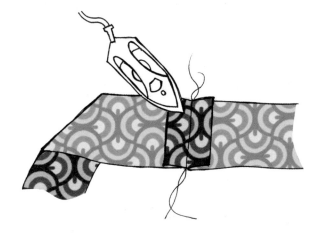

48

❷ PRESSING THE EDGES

Press under ³⁄₈" along each long edge of both strips.

❸ FUSING THE STRIPS

Place the backing strip on your ironing board with the right side face down. Unroll the fusible hem tape and position it centrally over the strip. Trim to length. Now lay the main fabric strip right side up and centered on top so that an equal margin of backing fabric peeps out along both sides.

❹ The fusible hem tape is now sandwiched between the two strips. Following the manufacturer's instructions, fuse the layers together, taking care to move the iron in an up-and-down pressing movement to keep strips in the right position.

❺ SEWING THE STRIPS TOGETHER

Thread the sewing machine with black thread. Sew the top layer in place by working a line of stitching ¹⁄₈" from each folded edge.

❻ MAKING THE HANDLE LOOP

Press under ⁵⁄₈" at each end. Fold back another 8" at one end for the loop and baste the first 1¹⁄₂" to the leash. Sew a 1¹⁄₄" rectangle at the end, then reinforce this by working two diagonal lines from corner to corner.

❼ ATTACHING THE CLIP

Slide the clip onto the leash so that it lies 1¹⁄₂" in from the end, then fold over and baste down the end of the leash. Sew down the folded end with a reinforced rectangle, as for the handle loop, stitching as close to the clip as you can.

HANGING BIRDS

*The Madauri cotton print collection
is perfect for these Indian-inspired
peacocks. You can stitch each one in
a different combination or make
a string of matching birds.*

YOU WILL NEED

- selection of small amounts of Liberty Madauri cotton in eight prints of your choice (we used Indira in colorways 4 and 5; Priya in colorways 2 and 8; Tehzeeb in colorways 3 and 6; and Zai in colorways 1 and 7)
- matching sewing thread
- tailor's chalk or air-erasable fabric pen
- safety-standard polyester toy stuffing
- 2¼ yd of ⅛"-wide waxed cord
- five ¾" and one ⅝" round beads
- large upholstery needle
- sewing kit
- sewing machine

TEMPLATES

Copy the template on page 155, enlarging it by 220% for bird 1, 200% for bird 2, 160% for bird 3, 140% for bird 4, and 120% for bird 5. Cut neatly around the outlines and number each template.

CUTTING OUT

from Liberty Madauri cotton prints

bird 1 tail	one 15¾"-x-9" rectangle
bird 2 tail	one 13¾"-x-8" rectangle
bird 3 tail	one 12"-x-7" rectangle
bird 4 tail	one 10"-x-5½" rectangle
bird 5 tail	one 8"-x-4¾" rectangle

PRIYA *is based on a bold one-color pattern that was designed especially for the Liberty spring/summer 2007 collection.*

❶ CUTTING OUT THE FIRST SIDE OF THE BODY

The bodies for all five birds are made in the same way. Start by pinning the body template to the wrong side of the fabric, then draw around the edge and cut out ¼" outside the outline. The drawn line is the stitching line.

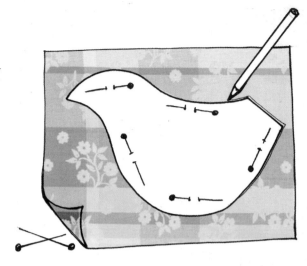

❷ SEWING AND STUFFING THE BODY

Pin the right side of the cut-out body to the right side of a piece of matching fabric, lining up the stripes and pattern. Stitch along the outline, leaving the tail open between template points A and B. Trim the seam allowance back to ⅛". Turn right side out through the opening, then fold ¼" inside around the opening and baste. Press lightly. Stuff the body, using a pencil to push small amounts of filling down into the head and neck.

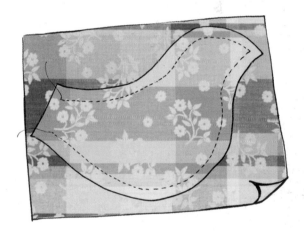

❸ STITCHING THE BIRD'S WINGS

The three largest birds have wings. Draw around the wing template onto the wrong side of the fabric, then cut out ¼" outside the outline. Pin to the right side of another piece of the print as for the body but without matching the pattern. Stitch all the way around the outline and trim the seam to ⅛". Carefully cut a ¾"–1¼" slit through the center back and turn the wing right side out through this opening. Reverse the template and make the second wing in the same way.

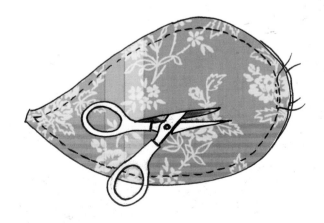

❹ JOINING THE WINGS TO THE BODY

Stuff the wings lightly with filling, pushing it right to the tips, then hand stitch the opening. Pin the wings to the body, making sure that they are both level and at the same angle, then sew securely in place between points C and D.

❺ MAKING AND PRESSING THE FANTAIL

With right sides together, fold the tail in half widthwise. Pin and seam the ends. Turn right side out and press. Mark the center top with a pin. Starting at this point, fold the fabric into a series of concertina pleats, pressing each one. When you

reach the end, unfold and press the other half from the center outward. Make the pleats ³/₄" wide for the largest bird, and progressively narrower for the others.

❻ SEWING THE TAIL TO THE BODY

Refold the tail and stab stitch the bottom ends of the pleats together to make a fan. Slot the tail into the tail opening. Stitch in place securely, using a thimble to push your needle all the way through the pleats.

❼ PUTTING IT ALL TOGETHER

Thread the waxed cord through the upholstery needle and pull it through the center top of the largest bird's body, close to the seam. Check that the bird hangs straight and alter the position of the cord if not. When it is balanced, pass the second end of the cord through the needle and thread on two beads. Make a knot 4" from the bird. Pass the needle up through the next bird, check the position and thread on two more beads. Add the other three birds in the same way. Finish off the thread in a loop for hanging.

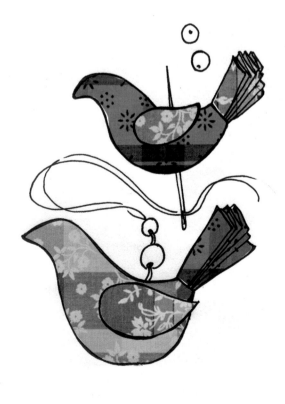

BASKET BAG

———— • ————

This ingenious bag can be used as a liner for a bicycle basket, but the additional handles allow you to lift out the bag and carry it with you. Team the bag with a matching saddle cover for a sweet ride (see page 61).

YOU WILL NEED

for the basket bag and saddle cover
- 1¼ yd of Liberty Tana Lawn in each of two prints of your choice for the main fabric and the lining fabric (we used Katie and Millie in colorway A and Travelling Threads in colorway C)
- 24" x 20" of plain cotton fabric, for the bag bases
- sheet of paper and pencil
- sheet of corrugated plastic to fit base of basket
- double-sided tape
- 16" x 12" of polyester batting
- air-erasable fabric pen and clear ruler
- 2½ yd of ¾"-wide bias binding
- 1¼ yd of ¼"-wide elastic each for bag and saddle
- matching sewing thread
- sewing machine
- sewing kit
- elastic threader or safety pin

NOTE

See page 61 for saddle cover instructions.

See page 61 for saddle cover instructions.

CUTTING OUT BASKET-BAG FABRIC PIECES

from Liberty Tana Lawn main print
one side piece
one base piece
handles   two 16"-x-6" rectangles

from Liberty Tana Lawn lining print
one side piece

from plain cotton fabric
one base piece

PREPARING BASKET-BAG PAPER PATTERN PIECES

for the side piece
width = circumference of basket + 4"
depth = height of basket + 4"

for the base
Trace around the basket base to make a paper template. Cut out ³⁄₈" within the line so the template lies ³⁄₈" inside the basket edge. Fold in four and mark the quarters with notches.

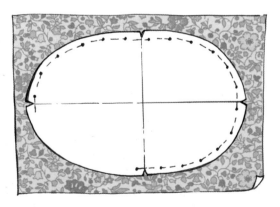

56

❶ PREPARING THE SIDE PIECE

Fold the main fabric side piece in half widthwise, then in half again. Mark the quarter sections by snipping ¼" notches into the lower edge, at the end of each fold. Pin the short edges with right sides together and machine stitch with a ³⁄₈" seam. Press the seam open.

❷ SEWING THE GATHERING STITCHES

Using a double length of thread, sew four lines of ¼" running stitches between the notches just under ³⁄₈" from the lower edge. Leave long tails at the end of each line of stitching.

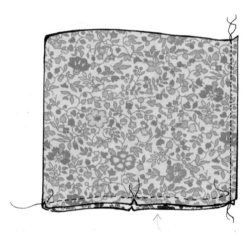

❸ JOINING ON THE BASE

With the right sides together, pin the lower edge of the seam to the notch on the top edge of the fabric-print base. Match up and pin the other notches.

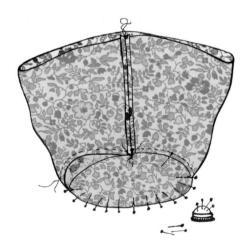

❹ Draw up the first gathering thread so that the edge of the side piece fits exactly along the first quarter of the base. Pin the two together, then do the same with the other three quarter sections. Baste, then machine stitch with a ³⁄₈" seam.

❺ Turn the bag right side out. Cut a plastic base piece using the template and place it inside the bag. Secure the plastic base in place with two strips of double-sided tape.

❻ ADDING THE LINING

Make the lining by repeating steps 1 to 4 with the lining fabric side piece and plain fabric base. Slip it inside the outer bag, with wrong sides together and matching the seams. Pin the two together along the bottom edge.

❼ Work a round of small running stitches close to the plastic, stitching through both layers of fabric.

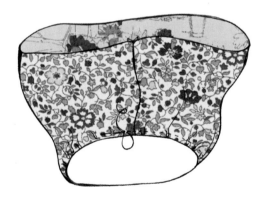

⑧ BINDING THE OPENING

Pin and baste the top edges of the inner and outer bags together. Fold the bias binding in half and slot it over the top edges, starting close to the seam line. Pin the binding in place all around the opening, then trim the end. Machine stitch close to the edge of the binding to make a channel for the elastic, leaving the last ³/₄" unstitched.

⑩ ADDING THE HANDLES

Pin the first handle to the bag so that both inside edges lie 2¹/₂" from the seam and the ends are 1¹/₄" down from the top edge. Baste, then machine stitch in place below the binding with a rectangle crossed by two diagonal lines. Add the second handle to the other side in the corresponding place.

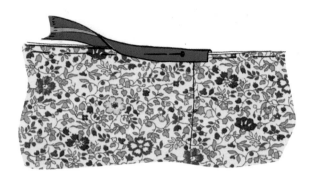

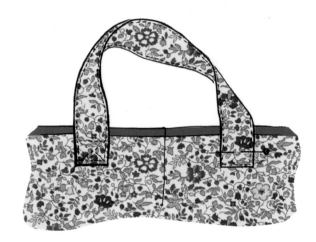

⑨ MAKING THE HANDLES

Press each handle piece in half lengthwise with the wrong sides together. Unfold and press over the long edges to meet the center crease. Press under ³/₈" at each end. Refold the crease, press once again and baste the edges together. Topstitch around all four edges of the handle.

⑪ THREADING THE ELASTIC

Thread the elastic through an elastic threader or pin a safety pin to one end. Ease the elastic through the opening and feed it all the way around the binding and out again. Pull up the ends slightly and slip the bag over the basket—the top edge should fit snugly but still be easy to remove. Check the fit, sew the two ends securely together, and trim. Push the join back through the opening and sew the loose end of binding in place.

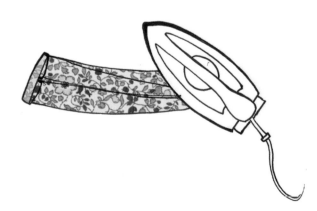

SADDLE COVER

Lightly padded for a more comfortable ride, this saddle cover is reversible so offers a choice of two different prints. A bicycle is simply underdressed without one.

CUTTING OUT
Cut one saddle cover from the main print and the lining print, and from the batting. Trim off ³/₈" all around from the batting.

TEMPLATE
Copy the template on page 150, enlarging it by 200%.

NOTE
See page 56 for what you will need for this cover.

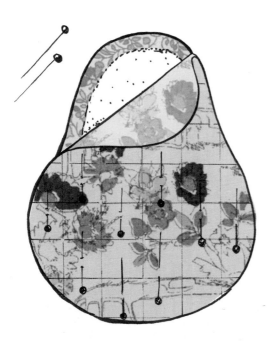

❶ MARKING THE QUILTING LINES
Fold one of the fabric saddle pieces in half lengthwise to find the center. Draw along this line using a clear ruler and an air-erasable fabric pen. Add more parallel lines on each side, spacing them 1¼" apart, then draw another set of lines across them, also 1¼" apart, to make a square grid.

❷ WORKING THE QUILTING
Place the main fabric saddle piece face down and center the batting on top of it. Position the lining fabric piece on top, right side up, matching the edges carefully. Pin all three layers together, between the vertical lines.

❸ Machine stitch along each of the vertical lines, then remove the pins and machine stitch along the horizontal lines.

❹ FINISHING OFF
Finish the edge with bias binding and add the elastic as for steps 8 and 11 of the bicycle basket bag. Pull up the elastic tightly enough to make the cover a secure fit around the bicycle saddle.

CAFETIERE COVER AND COASTERS

— • —

*Add a shot of color to the breakfast table
with a padded cafetière cozy.
By using the same method, you can
make a set of four coordinating coasters.*

YOU WILL NEED

- 36" x 8" of Liberty Tana Lawn in print of your choice for the main fabric (we used Farhad in colorway D)
- 36" x 8" of quilt batting
- 36" x 8" of plain cotton fabric, for the backing
- 4½ yd of ½"-wide bias binding in a complementary color
- two ¾" hook-and-loop circles
- two ¾" buttons
- matching sewing thread
- dressmaker's graph paper
- sewing machine
- sewing kit

NOTE

If you only want to make the cafetière cover (without the four coasters), you will need 14" x 8" each of the main fabric, the batting, and the backing.

PREPARING PAPER PATTERN PIECE FOR COVER
The cover is designed for a standard 8-cup or 1-liter cafetière. Copy the template on page 151, enlarging it by 200%. Cut out the paper pattern piece and check the size of the cover against your cafetière before cutting the fabric. You can then adjust the height or width if necessary.

TEMPLATES
Copy the templates on page 151 for the cafetière cover and tabs, enlarging them by 200%.

FARHAD *was inspired by Art Nouveau repeats and mazes of stately gardens in Vienna. The design captures motifs from both art and nature.*

③ QUILTING THE LAYERS

Thread the machine with matching sewing thread. Starting parallel to the right edge, sew a series of vertical lines, 3/8" apart, across the entire surface. Keep the right hand edge of the presser foot lined up with the previous row of stitches so that the lines are spaced regularly. Start each row from the top edge to prevent the fabric from puckering.

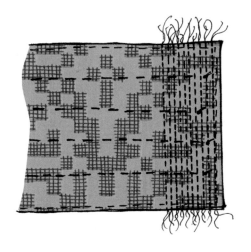

① LAYERING THE FABRICS

Spread the batting across the plain fabric and place the main fabric on top, with the right side face up. Align the corners and pin all three layers together around the outside edge.

④ CUTTING OUT THE SHAPES

Using the paper templates, cut out the cafetière cover and two tabs from the quilted fabric. Then cut four 5½" squares with gently rounded corners for the set of coasters.

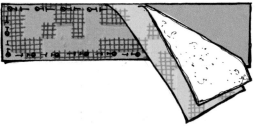

② WORKING THE BASTING

Using a contrasting thread, baste around all four edges. Now sew four lines of basting stitches, about 1½" apart, along the width. This will stop the fabrics from sliding when they are being quilted.

❺ BINDING THE EDGES

Open out one end of the binding and turn back the first ³⁄₈". Refold the creases. With right sides facing and raw edges aligned, pin this end to the left edge of the cafetière cover, about 2" up from the bottom corner. Baste the binding to the cover, gently stretching the raw edge to fit around the curves. Leave a ³⁄₈" overlap at the end and trim.

❽ SEWING THE TABS TO THE COVER

With the right sides face down, pin the plain ends of the tabs to the left edge of the cover, so that they overlap by 1¹⁄₂". Wrap the cover around your cafetière and slip the tabs through the handle. Adjust the positions if you need to, then baste the tabs in place. Machine stitch them in place from the right side, sewing to within ¹⁄₈" of the binding.

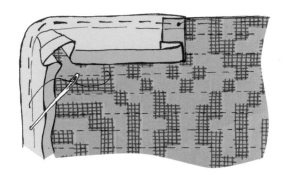

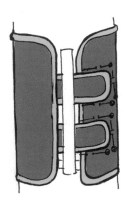

❻ Machine stitch ¹⁄₈" from the edge, slowing right down at the corners for accuracy. Turn the binding to the wrong side and slipstitch the folded edge to the back of the cover. Bind the tabs and the coasters in the same way.

❼ ADDING THE BUTTONS

Stick the hooked side of the hook-and-loop circles to the wrong side of the tabs. Hand stitch them in place. Sew the buttons securely to the right side, directly above the dots.

❾ FINISHING THE TAB FASTENINGS

Put the cover back on the cafetière, with the right side outward. Pin the tabs to the right edge, so that the cover fits snugly. Mark the position of each one with three more pins, then take out the first pins. Stick the looped sides of the hook-and-loop circles in place between the pins and stitch them on securely.

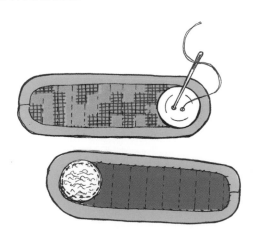

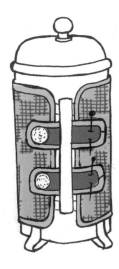

DRUM LAMPSHADE

A minimal amount of fabric can provide maximum impact when used to cover a simple drum lampshade. When light passes through the fabric, Liberty prints take on a luminous quality.

YOU WILL NEED

Liberty Tana Lawn in three different prints and colorways of your choice:
- 53" x 8" of main print 1 (we used Scilly Flora in colorway B)
- 53" x 4" of complementary print 2 (we used Scilly Flora in colorway C)
- 53" x 6" of complementary print 3 (we used Jugenstil in colorway C)
- ³/₈"-wide double-sided tape
- matching sewing thread
- sewing kit
- plain cardboard drum lampshade, 10" tall, 15³/₄" in diameter, and with a circumference of 49¹/₄"

CUTTING OUT

The measurements given below are for the specified lampshade: adjust the size of your fabric strips accordingly to fit a different shape. Add 1¹/₄" to the depth of both top and bottom strips and ³/₄" to the depth of the center strips. The length of each strip should equal the diameter of your shade, plus an extra 1¹/₄".

from print 1
one 50¹/₂"-x-2¹/₂" strip
one 50¹/₂"-x-4¹/₂" strip

from print 2
one 50¹/₂"-x-3¹/₄" strip

from print 3
one 50¹/₂"-x-2³/₄" strip
one 50¹/₂"-x-2" strip

SCILLY FLORA *is a tropical multicolored design that was inspired by the wonderful flora of the Tresco Abbey Garden.*

❶ MAKING THE COVER

Press the strips and lay them out in their final order. Pin the top two with right sides together, then machine stitch, leaving a ³/₈" seam allowance. Press the seam open. Add the remaining three strips in the same way.

❷ Trim the side edges so that they are perfectly straight. Baste them with right sides together, leaving a ⁵/₈" seam allowance. Slip the cover over the shade to check the size: it should fit snugly with a ³/₄" overlap at the top and bottom. Remove the cover and adjust if necessary. Machine stitch the seam and press it open. Turn right side out.

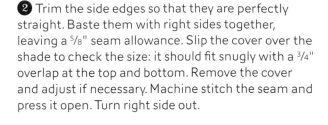

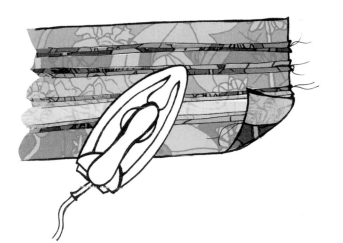

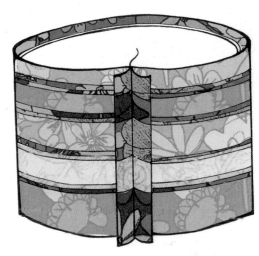

❸ STICKING THE COVER IN PLACE

Slip the cover back over the lampshade so that the seam allowances project equally at the top and bottom edges.

❹ Stick a round of double-sided tape to the inside of the shade, just inside the top edge. Peel off the backing paper. Fold the seam allowance over and press it onto the adhesive. Do the same at the bottom edge.

CHEVRON QUILT

If the word "patchwork" conjures up images of folksy throws then think again. This contemporary, graphic design is deceptively easy to stitch yet is an excellent introduction to core patchwork techniques.

YOU WILL NEED

Liberty Lifestyle craft fabric in five coordinating prints of your choice:
- 44" x 28" in print 1 (we used Mackintosh in colorway B)
- 44" x 28" in print 2 (we used Newbury in colorway B)
- 44" x 28" in print 3 (we used Herbert in colorway B)
- 44" x 24" in print 4 (we used Wells in colorway B)
- 44" x 44" in print 5 (we used Lowke in colorway B)
- 3³/₄ yd of 44"-wide white cotton fabric

- 79" x 87" of cotton or bamboo quilt batting
- 81"-x-95" white sheet, for the backing
- cutting mat and rotary cutter
- 6" quilter's square (see note)
- long ruler
- pencil
- quilter's curved safety pins
- white quilting thread
- matching sewing thread
- sewing machine
- sewing kit

FINISHED SIZE

The finished quilt measures approximately 69³/₄" x 81¹/₂".

NOTE

Quilter's squares are marked in ¹/₄", ¹/₂", and 1" squares. The quilt is built up of simple 6" blocks, each made from one white and one blue rectangle. The quickest way to prepare these is by rotary piecing as shown, but alternatively you can join two 6"-x-3¹/₄" pieces, with a ¹/₄" seam, by either hand or machine to make the block.

HERBERT *is based on a Liberty design from the early 1900s, when Liberty was renowned for its iconic Art Nouveau designs.*

❶ SEAMING THE STRIPS

Tear off a 4"-wide strip of white fabric and of fabric print, tearing them each from selvage to selvage. With right sides together, pin the strips along one long edge. Machine stitch, leaving a ³⁄₈" seam allowance, then press the seam toward the patterned fabric.

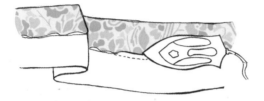

❷ CUTTING OUT THE BLOCKS

Place the joined strips, right side up, on a cutting mat. Position the 6" quilter's square on top, with the center 3" marking directly over the seam line. Carefully cut along each side of the square with a rotary cutter. You will need to make 38 blocks with each of prints 1, 2, 3, and 4, and 29 blocks with print 5. Cut nine 6"-x-3¼" rectangles from print 5 for the top edge and nine from white fabric for the bottom edge.

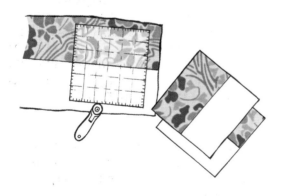

❸ LAYING OUT THE BLOCKS

All the blocks are set "on point" (diagonally). Starting at the top edge, lay out a horizontal row of ten print 5 blocks with the print at the top left. Add the next row of nine print 1 blocks, with the print at the bottom left. Now add ten more print 1 blocks with the print at the top left. Continue adding rows of nine or ten blocks in this way, grading the colors from dark to light: print 2, print 3, then print 4. Repeat the sequence of five zigzag stripes—print 5, print 1, print 2, print 3, and print 4. Add the print 5 rectangles at the top and the white rectangles at the bottom.

❹ SEWING ON THE RECTANGLES

Join the rectangles along the top edge of the quilt top to the blocks in the row directly below. With right sides together, pin the rectangle to the top right edge of the block. Machine stitch with a ¼" seam, then press the seam allowance over the rectangle. Sew the rectangles along the bottom edge of the quilt to the bottom left of the blocks above them.

❺ JOINING THE BLOCKS INTO ROWS

The blocks are stitched together in diagonal rows to make four large triangular sections. These are then joined up to make a rectangle. Start at the top right corner of the top triangle. Join the ten blocks that make up the right edge of the triangle, with 1/4" seam allowances. Press the seam allowances away from the white fabric. Now join the nine blocks that make up the next row in the same way.

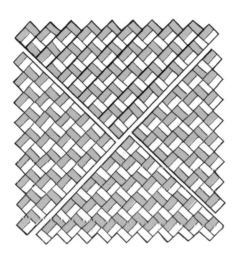

❻ JOINING THE ROWS TOGETHER

Pin the two rows with right sides together. Match the left edges and insert a pin at each of the points where the seams meet. Machine stitch 1/4" from the edge, stopping the seam 1/4" from the end of the final rectangle at the outside top edge of the quilt.

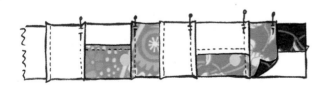

❼ PRESSING THE SEAMS

Press back a 1/4" along the edge of the rectangle and press the long seam allowance downward, over the first row. This will give you a pre-finished top edge when you complete the quilt. Sew together the remaining diagonal rows in the same way until the top triangular section is assembled.

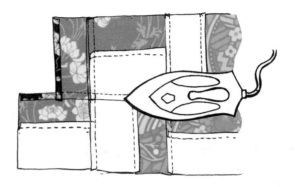

❽ ASSEMBLING THE OTHER SECTIONS

Sew together the left triangular section, starting with the bottom right row of blocks and matching up the right edge of each row. You can stitch the seams between these rows from edge to edge (without stopping 1/4" from the outside edge of the quilt). Join the rows in the right triangular section as for the left triangular section. Then join together the bottom triangular section, finishing the bottom edge in the same way as the top edge.

❾ Join the top section to the left section and the right section to the bottom section. Press the seams to one side, then join the two large triangles to complete the quilt top.

🔟 TRIMMING THE EDGES

Now trim off the surplus fabric to straighten the side edges. Place a long ruler along the right edge of the quilt top, in line with the inside corners. Draw a pencil line along the ruler, then continue down to the bottom corner. Do the same on the left edge and cut along both lines.

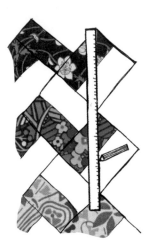

⓫ LAYERING THE QUILT

Press the backing sheet and spread it out over the floor. Spread the batting centrally on top, then lay the quilt top, right side up, centrally over the two layers. Starting at one edge and working across the quilt, pin the layers together with quilter's curved safety pins. Position them in a regular grid at intervals of about 6".

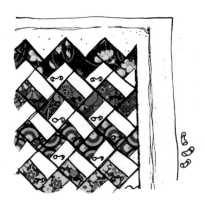

⓬ WORKING THE HAND QUILTING

Using white thread, sew lines of short running stitches along the top and bottom edges of each white zigzag, 1/4" from the seam lines.

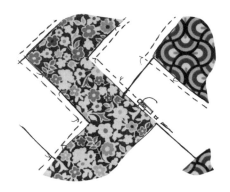

⓭ REMOVING THE SURPLUS FABRIC

Baste along the side edges, then trim off the surplus batting and backing in line with the edge of the patchwork. Trim the batting at the top and bottom in line with the folded edge. Cut away the surplus backing following the zigzag edge, but leaving a 3/8" margin as the seam allowance.

⓮ FINISHING THE TOP AND BOTTOM EDGES

Make a small snip into the margin at each inside corner. Baste the backing to the patchwork, turning the seam allowance inward (over the batting), so the two folded edges match exactly. Slipstitch the edges together using dark sewing thread.

⓯ BINDING THE SIDE EDGES

Cut four 44"-x-2" strips from the remaining print 5. With right sides together, join the short ends and press the seams open. Bind the side edges as given for the striped throw on page 148.

TABLE MATS

———•———

*Introduce color and pattern to your
table settings with these roll-up mats.
Slot your cutlery neatly into the integral
pockets with a contrast-bound edge.*

YOU WILL NEED

for each mat
- 24" x 16" of Liberty Tana Lawn in each of two complementary prints of your choice (we used Mitsi in colorway B and Glenjade in colorway N)
- 24" x 16" of medium-weight iron-on interfacing
- matching sewing thread
- sewing machine
- sewing kit

PREPARING THE FABRIC

Decide which fabric will be uppermost and iron the interfacing to the wrong side of it.

CUTTING OUT

Use a rotary cutter, quilter's square and cutting mat for accuracy, or make a template from dressmaker's graph paper.

from each Liberty Tana Lawn print

for each mat   one 17³/₄"-x-12" rectangle
for each pocket   one 3¹/₄"-x-6¹/₄" rectangle

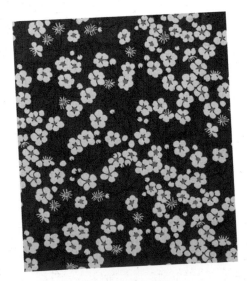

MITSI *is based on a design created by the Liberty studio during the
1950s. With its Japanese-style cherry blossom, it plays on Liberty's history.*

② CLIPPING THE CORNERS

At each corner, measure and mark two points, each ³/₈" from the corner, and draw a line between them. Snip along this line. This may cut into the stitches; don't worry as any gap will be folded into the border.

① JOINING THE TWO LAYERS

Pin the two rectangles together with the right sides facing outward. Machine stitch around the outside edge, leaving a ³/₈" seam allowance. Trim the seam allowance to ¹/₄".

③ TURNING THE EDGES

With the stiffened fabric uppermost, fold ¹/₄" to the front along each edge and press, using the tip of the iron. Repeat so that you have a double ¹/₄" hem all around and the raw edges are concealed.

❹ SEWING DOWN THE HEM

Using a matching thread, machine stitch the hem, stitching along the center of the hem. The narrow pressed hem should stay in place as you stitch, so won't need any pins or basting.

❺ MAKING THE POCKET

Pin the two pockets pieces with right sides together and machine stitch with a ¼" seam allowance, leaving a 2" openinge in the center of one long edge. Press back the seam allowance on either side of the opening. Clip the corners to lessen the bulk and turn right side out.

❻

Ease out the right angles and press lightly. Turn 1½" of the contrasting side over to the front of the pocket to make a cuff and press this fold.

❼ SEWING ON THE POCKET

Position the pocket ¾" up from the bottom edge of the mat and ¾" in from the right edge. Pin, then machine topstitch in place ⅛" from the edges, keeping the top open for the cutlery. Reinforce both ends of the topstitching with reverse stitches to keep the pocket securely in place.

"LIBBY" DOLL

Every girl adores a Liberty print outfit, and Libby the doll is no different. Because of the small parts, like the shoes, this toy is not suitable for a child under 4 years old.

YOU WILL NEED

- 20" x 12" of cream linen fabric
- 3½ ounces of safety-standard polyester toy filling
- six-strand cotton embroidery floss in black and pink, for the eyes and mouth
- small ball of brown wool yarn, for the hair
- elasticated hair band, for the hair
- selection of remnants of Liberty Tana Lawn in an assortment of different prints
- 2¾"-x-¼" strip of hook-and-loop tape
- 14" square of felt
- 6" x 2½" of iron-on fusible bonding web
- three small buttons
- matching sewing thread
- sewing machine
- sewing kit
- 8" square of cardboard
- knitting needle
- blunt-tipped tapestry needle

TEMPLATES

Copy the templates on page 152, enlarging them by 200%, and cut out the body, arm, leg, bodice, jacket, and shoe paper pattern pieces.

CUTTING OUT

from cream linen fabric
FOR THE DOLL
two bodies
two legs (cut on fold)
two arms (cut on fold)

from assorted Liberty Tana Lawn prints
FOR THE DRESS BODICE
two 10"-x-8" rectangles
FOR THE DRESS SKIRT RUFFLES
two 2½"-x-19¾" rectangles
two 3¼"-x-19¾" rectangles
two 4"-x-19¾" rectangles
two 4¾"-x-19¾" rectangles
FOR THE DRESS SASH
one 3¼"-x-15¾" strip

from felt
FOR THE JACKET
two 10"-x-6" rectangles
FOR THE SHOES
one 2½"-x-5" rectangle (fuse this felt rectangle to a scrap of a fabric print using bonding web, following the manufacturer's instructions)

making the doll

❶ MAKING THE HEAD AND BODY
Referring to the template, mark the features, hairline, and points A, B, and C on one of the body pieces. With right sides together, pin and baste the two body pieces together. Machine stitch twice around the head and shoulders from points A to A, to reinforce the seam line. Stitch both side edges between points B and C, working a few reverse stitches at each end to secure the seams.

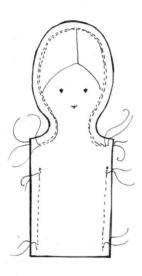

❷ FINISHING OFF THE SEAMS
Trim the seam allowance around the head and shoulders to 1/4". Clip a row of small triangles into the seam allowance, cutting to within 1/8" of the stitching. Space the notches 1/4" apart along the neck curves and 3/8" apart around the head. Press back the seam allowance at the side and bottom edges of the body, on both front and back.

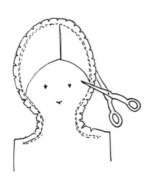

❸ SEWING THE LEGS AND ARMS
Refold the arms and legs and baste the edges together. Machine stitch these seams, leaving a 3/8" seam allowance, once again reinforcing both ends. Trim the seam allowance to 1/4", tapering it down to 1/8" at the narrow ends.

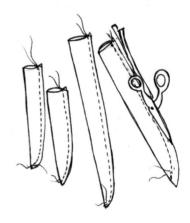

❹ TURNING RIGHT SIDE OUT
Turn all the parts right side out, using a knitting needle to push the limbs through. Ease out the seams by rolling them between your fingers and thumbs so that the stitches lie at the outside edges.

❺ STUFFING THE DOLL

Stuff all the doll parts firmly, using the knitting needle to push the toy filling right down into the hands and feet and up through the neck into the head. Make sure that the neck is stuffed well before filling the body, to ensure that the head will stay upright. Baste across the top edge of the arms and legs, with the seam lines at the center back.

❻ ADDING THE LEGS AND ARMS

Slip the top of the legs into the bottom of the body. Pin and baste in place, then hand stitch with matching thread, sewing securely through all the layers. Insert the top of the arms into the side openings, in line with the shoulders. Sew in place as for the legs.

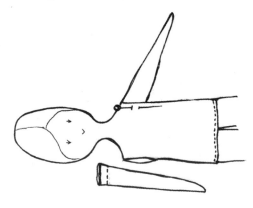

❼ EMBROIDERING THE FEATURES

Using black cotton embroidery floss, sew a ⅛" vertical black stitch for each eye, with a shorter stitch at a slight angle either side for the eyelashes. Make the mouth with a short pink straight stitch caught in the middle with a small stitch to turn it into a smile. Add a little real blusher to give her rosy cheeks.

❽ MAKING THE HAIR

Draw a 6" line along the center front of the cardboard and wind the wool yarn evenly at right angles to the line until it is covered by the yarn. Cut a length of yarn from the end and thread it through a tapestry needle. Sew a row of backstitches along the center line: this will be the doll's hair part. Cut through the yarn along the center back of the cardboard.

❾ STYLING THE HAIR

Pin the stitched line along the part marked on the template and down the center back of the head. Using matching thread, hand stitch in place along the part. Stitch the front hair in place either side of the face with a strand of wool and trim to the same length all around. Gather it into a low ponytail and secure with a hair band. Divide this in two just above the band and tuck the loose ends up through the gap.

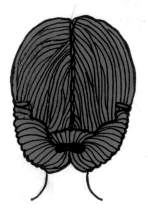

making the dress

❶ MAKING THE BODICE

Place the two fabric-print rectangles with right sides together, then pin on the bodice template. Carefully machine stitch around the side and top of the paper, leaving the bottom edge open. Cut out, leaving a ¼" seam allowance along the stitching and ⅜" along the bottom edge. Clip into the seam allowance as for the doll's head. Press up ⅜" around the bottom edge. Turn right side out and press lightly.

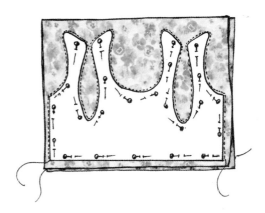

❷ PREPARING THE SKIRT RUFFLES

Pin the first pair of fabric-print rectangles with right sides together and sew along the side and bottom edges. Clip the corners, turn right side out, and press. Set your machine to the longest straight stitch and sew two lines of stitching along the raw-edged top of the ruffle, ¼" down from the top edge and ¼" apart, leaving long ends. Prepare the remaining three ruffles in the same way.

❸ ASSEMBLING THE SKIRT

Find the two top threads (one from each row of stitching) at one corner of the first ruffle and gently pull them, while with your other hand gathering up the fabric. When you have gathered half the rectangle, repeat from the other end. Adjust the gathers until the ruffle measures 8" wide.

❹ Do the same with the other three ruffles, then layer them on top of each other, with the longest ruffle at the bottom. Baste the top edges of the ruffles together and machine zigzag stitch through all the gathers.

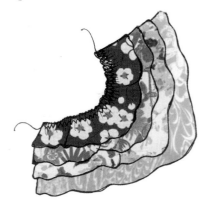

❺ JOINING THE SKIRT TO THE BODICE

Slip the zigzagged skirt edge between the front and back layers of the bodice, then pin and baste it in place. Machine stitch through all the layers: this seam doesn't have to be perfect as it will be concealed by the sash.

❻ SEWING THE SASH

Fold the sash strip in half lengthwise with right sides together. Pin the raw edges together and machine stitch ⅜" from the edge, leaving a 2" opening in the center of the long edge and angling the seams at the short edges to create points. Press back the seam allowance either side of the opening, trim the corners, turn right side out, and press. Slipstitch the opening closed. Hand stitch the sash to the top of the skirt so it conceals the seam line.

❼ FINISHING OFF

Separate the two halves of the hook-and-loop strip and machine stitch one half to each side of the bodice opening at the back of the dress. Place the dress on the doll, press the hook-and-loop strips together to do up the bodice, and double knot the shoulder and waist ties.

making the flower

❶ Fuse a scrap of a fabric print to a scrap of felt for a little flower. Using pinking shears, cut out a ⅝" circle. Sew a button in the center and sew to the doll's hair.

making the jacket

❶ Place the two felt rectangles together and pin on the template. Again following the edge of the paper closely, stitch the shoulder, side, and underarm seams. Secure both ends of the stitched lines with a few reverse stitches. Cut out ⅛" from the stitching lines, then cut along the template along the bottom edge. Cut up the center front of the jacket and turn right side out.

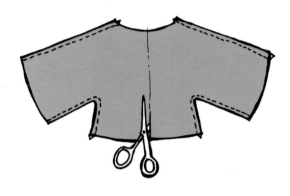

making the shoes

❶ Cut the bonded felt and fabric print into two 2½" squares. Fold one in half, with the felt facing inward, and pin the template along the fold. Draw around the outline, then machine stitch along the sole. Snip out the semicircle, cut along the instep, and trim the seam to ⅛". Turn right side out, fit onto the doll's foot, and stitch on securely. Sew a small button to the outside edge. Make the other shoe in the same way.

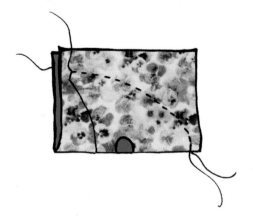

FLORAL GARLAND

This impossibly pretty floral garland is not just exceptionally simple to make, it also is an effective way to use up leftover scraps of fabric from other projects.

YOU WILL NEED

- selection of remnants of Liberty Tana Lawn in an assortment of different prints, including a green colorway for the leaves
- iron-on fusible bonding web
- one or two buttons for each flower center
- six-strand cotton embroidery floss
- air-erasable fabric pen or chalk pencil
- pinking shears
- sewing thread
- sewing machine
- sewing kit

TEMPLATES

Copy the templates on page 150, enlarging them by 200%, and cut out the inner and outer flowers, the center circle, and the leaf templates.

PREPARING THE FABRIC BEFORE CUTTING OUT

The three layers that make up each flower are all double-sided, with a different fabric print on the front and back fused together with fusible bonding web. The leaves are also double-sided. To prepare the bonded fabric, choose two different prints of similar size and press a same-shaped piece of fusible bonding web to the wrong side of the first fabric, following the manufacturer's instructions. Peel off the backing paper and iron the adhesive side to the wrong side of the second fabric.

CUTTING OUT

Draw around the edges of the flower and leaf templates directly onto the double-sided bonded fabric using an air-erasable fabric pen or chalk pencil. Neatly cut out each shape. Use pinking shears to cut out the center circles and leaves.

FOR ONE YARD OF GARLAND YOU WILL NEED

from assorted Liberty Tana Lawn prints
four outer flowers
four inner flowers
four center circles (cut out with pinking shears)
2"-wide strips in various lengths (4"–10"), for the garland string

from green Liberty Tana Lawn print
three leaves (cut out with pinking shears)

❶ ASSEMBLING A FLOWER

Position the inner flower on top of the outer flower so that the petals sit alternately, then place the center circle in the middle. Using all six strands of embroidery floss, sew them together at the center point with a few small stitches, then pass the needle through to the back.

❷ Fold the flower into quarters. Stitch three or four times through the tip of the fold to hold the layers together and to give the flower its three-dimensional quality.

❸ ADDING THE CENTER BUTTON

Open out the flower and sew one or two buttons securely to the center using all six strands of a contrasting embroidery floss.

❹ MAKING THE GARLAND STRING

Pin the short ends of two 2"-wide strips with right sides together. Machine stitch leaving a ³⁄₈" seam, then press the seam open. Continue adding more strips until you have the required garland length, then press the seams open.

❺ Press the garland string in half lengthwise, so that the seams are on the inside, then unfold. Turn and press one long edge inward so that it lies along the center crease.

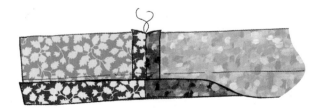

❻ Press a similar turning along the other edge, then refold the center and press the garland string in half. Sew the folded edges together ¹⁄₈" from the edge.

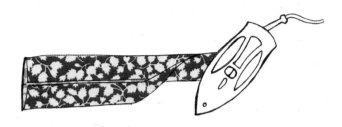

❼ PUTTING THE GARLAND TOGETHER

Now decide on the order of the flowers, placing them alongside the garland string at approximately 10" intervals. Securely hand stitch the folded tip of each flower to the string, using a double length of sewing thread. Tie the leaves to the string in the gaps between the flowers.

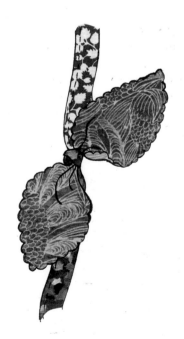

STORAGE BOLSTER

Storing your winter duvet can be a bit of a problem, but this beautiful velvet bolster can solve your dilemma and add some glamor to your bedroom.

YOU WILL NEED

- 40" square of Liberty cotton velvet in print of your choice (we used Felix Raison in colorway A)
- 40" square of medium-weight plain cotton fabric
- 2¼ yd of 1¼"-wide velvet ribbon, for the trim
- 2¼ yd of ¾"-wide velvet ribbon, for the ties
- matching sewing thread
- sewing machine
- sewing kit
- large safety pin

CUTTING OUT

from Liberty cotton velvet print
one 36¼" square

from plain cotton fabric
two 7"-x-36¼" rectangles
two 8¾"-x-36¼" rectangles

The finished stuffed bolster is approximately 53¼" long. Adjust the width of the velvet panel to make it longer or shorter.

PREPARING THE FABRIC PIECES
Finish all four raw edges of each fabric piece with a machine zigzag or overlock stitch.

FELIX RAISON *was inspired by a Liberty dress fabric design that was based on an 1850s paisley shawl drawing found in the Liberty archive.*

❶ MARKING THE RIBBON CHANNELS

Press under 2" along one long edge of each 7"-wide plain cotton rectangle, then unfold. These hems will later form the gathering channels for the ribbon ties.

❷ JOINING THE PLAIN COTTON RECTANGLES

With right sides together, pin the uncreased long edges of the 7" rectangles to the 8¾" rectangles. Baste together and machine stitch ⅝" from the edge. Press the seam allowances open.

❹ TRIMMING THE SEAMS WITH RIBBON

Press the seams open. To avoid damaging the velvet, lay a clean towel over your ironing board to protect the fabric's pile and press lightly from the wrong side. Cut the 1¼" ribbon in half, then pin and securely baste one length centrally over each of the two seams between the velvet and the plain cotton. Using matching thread, machine stitch both edges from top to bottom, to prevent the ribbon from puckering.

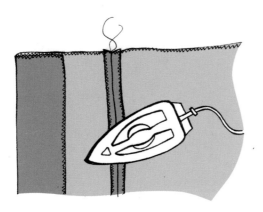

❸ ASSEMBLING THE BOLSTER

Pin the other long edges of the 8¾" rectangles, with right sides together, to the side edges of the velvet square. Baste the seams securely with two lines of ⅜" stitches to minimize any movement between the fabrics when they are sewn together. Machine stitch ⅜" from the edge, sewing both seams from top to bottom. If the velvet now projects below the cotton rectangles, simply trim off the excess fabric and refinish the edge.

❺ MAKING THE TUBE

Fold the completed cover in half lengthwise with right sides together. Pin the long edges together, carefully matching the ends of the ribbon and the other two seam lines. Work two lines of basting as before. Mark a point 3½" from each end, then stitch between these points, leaving a ⅝" seam allowance. Reinforce both ends of this seam.

❻ PRESSING THE LONG SEAM

Roll up the towel and place it inside the cover to protect the velvet. Gently press the whole seam allowance open with the tip of your iron.

❼ MAKING THE RIBBON CHANNELS

Baste down the unstitched seam allowances at each end and machine stitch ¼" from the folds.

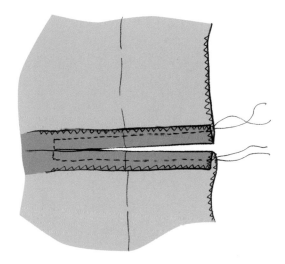

❽ Refold the 2" hems at each end, then pin and baste them in place all around the tube. Starting at the seam line, machine stitch ⅜" from the inner fold. Reinforce the slit opening by stitching backward and forward across the point where the seam meets up.

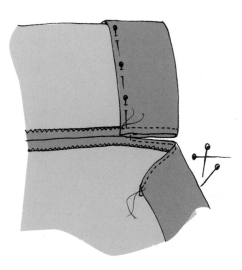

❾ THREADING THE RIBBONS THROUGH THE CHANNELS

Turn the bolster right side out. Cut the ¾" ribbon in half and fasten a large safety pin to the end of one length. Feed the pin through one ribbon channel, then thread the second length through the other end.

❿ STUFFING THE BOLSTER WITH YOUR DUVET

Roll the duvet up tightly from top to bottom. Push one end as far into the bolster as you can, then pull it through from the other end: having a helper will speed up the process. Pull up the ribbons tightly, knot them, and tie them in a bow.

LEAF PILLOWS

Appliqué is a quick yet effective technique for producing decorative effects with fabric. Graphic shapes that are not too fine, like this leaf silhouette, work best.

YOU WILL NEED

for the large pillow

- 24" x 16" of Liberty Tana Lawn in print of your choice (we used Wiltshire in colorway P), for the appliqué
- 24½" x 16½" of old gold linen, for the pillow front
- 28" x 18" of black linen, for the pillow back
- 14" zipper
- 24" x 16" of iron-on fusible bonding web
- 24"-x-16" pillow form

for the small pillow

- 18" x 12" of Liberty Tana Lawn in print of your choice (we used Lodden in colorway D or Felix and Isabelle in colorway D), for the appliqué
- 18½" x 12½" of black or olive green linen, for the pillow front
- 22" x 14" of old gold linen, for the pillow back
- 10" zipper
- 18" x 12" of iron-on fusible bonding web
- 18"-x-12" pillow form

CUTTING OUT

from black linen

wide back panel	one 21"-x-16½" rectangle
narrow back panel	one 5"-x-16½" strip

CUTTING OUT

from old gold linen

wide back panel	one 15¾"-x-12½" rectangle
narrow back panel	one 4¼"-x-12½" strip

for both size pillows
- sharp pencil
- matching sewing thread
- contrasting sewing thread
- sewing machine
- sewing kit

TEMPLATES

Copy the templates on page 153, enlarging them by 400%, and cut out the small pillow leaves and large pillow leaves paper pattern pieces.

The large and small pillows are made in the same way, regardless of size.

❶ CUTTING OUT THE APPLIQUÉ LEAVES

Enlarge the appropriate template on page 153 and trace the outline onto the paper side of the fusible bonding web. Roughly cut out and iron the adhesive side onto the back of the floral fabric, following the manufacturer's instructions. Neatly cut out along the pencil line.

❷ FUSING THE LEAVES TO THE PILLOW FRONT

Gently peel off the backing paper and position the leaf across the pillow front. Fuse it in place with a dry iron, using a pressing rather than a gliding action so it doesn't distort the fabric.

❸ FINISHING THE APPLIQUÉ EDGES

Set the machine controls to a narrow blanket or zigzag stitch. Using sewing thread to match or contrast with the floral fabric, sew all the way around the outside edge of the leaf motif. Carefully follow the contours to conceal the raw edges.

❹ JOINING THE BACK PANELS

Pin one long edge of the narrow strip to one short edge of the wide back panel, with right sides together. Machine stitch ¾" from the edge for 1½" at each end of the seam, securing each line of stitching with a few reverse stitches at the start and end. Baste the center of the seam together.

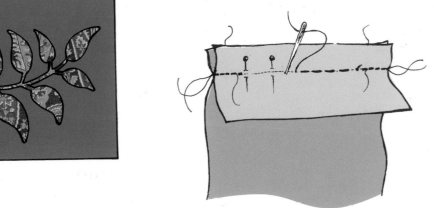

❺ ADDING THE ZIPPER

Press the seam open. Lay the right side of the zipper centrally across the seam allowances so that the teeth are in line with the seam and baste it securely in place.

❻

Now fit a zipper foot to your machine and thread it with matching sewing thread. Working from the right side, stitch around the zipper, ¼" from the seam line. Carefully remove the basting stitches and open the zipper.

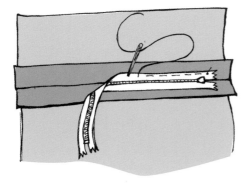

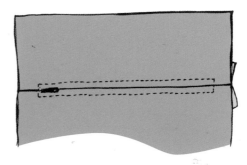

❼ FINISHING THE COVER

Pin the front to the back pieces, with right sides together and corners aligned, then machine stitch all the way around, ³/₈" from the outside edge. Trim the seam to ¼" and finish the raw edges with a machine overlock or zigzag stitch. Turn the cover right side out and lightly press. Insert the pillow from and close the zipper.

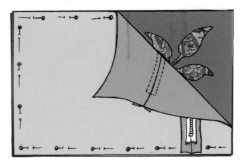

LODDEN *is an original William Morris design, first produced by Morris & Co. in 1884.*

EDGED PILLOWCASES

*The fine, high thread count of Liberty
Tana Lawn gives the fabric a luxurious,
silky feel while remaining durable,
which makes it perfect for a pillowcase.*

YOU WILL NEED

for a pair of pillowcases
- 53" x 40" of Liberty Tana Lawn in print of your choice for the main fabric (we used May Rose in colorway B)
- 53" x 40" of Liberty Tana Lawn in print of your choice for the coordinating fabric (we used Saeed in colorway A)
- 44" x 20" of plain white cotton fabric
- dressmaker's graph paper
- matching sewing thread
- sewing machine
- sewing kit

TEMPLATE

Copy the template on page 153, enlarging it by 200%, and cut out the scallop edge paper pattern piece.

CUTTING OUT

To allow for shrinkage, launder the fabric at 104°F and press well before cutting out. When cutting out, retain the selvage edge on at least one 20" edge of the main pillowcase pieces.

from Liberty Tana Lawn main print
main pillowcase	one 53"-x-20" rectangle
scallop edging	two 6"-x-20" strips
striped border	two $1^3/_8$"-x-20" strips

from Liberty Tana Lawn coordinating print
main pillowcase	one 53"-x-20" rectangle
scallop edging	two 6"-x-20" strips
striped border	two $1^3/_8$"-x-20" strips

from plain white cotton fabric
cuff	two $13^3/_4$"-x-20" rectangles
striped border	six $1^3/_8$"-x-20" strips

MAY ROSE *was hand-drawn from sunflowers to represent the annual worldwide sunflower planting by the Guerilla Gardeners on 1st May.*

❶ MAKING THE SCALLOP EDGING

Place one scallop edging strip of each of the fabric prints with right sides together and lay the paper pattern piece centrally on top. Pin it in place, positioning the pins about ³/₄" in from the edge. Machine stitch slowly along the scallops, carefully following the curved edge of the paper template.

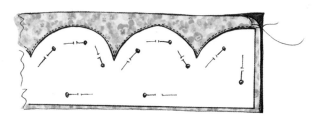

❷ Trim the straight side edges in line with the template, then remove the pins. Trim the seam allowance along the curved scalloped edge to ¹/₈". Snip vertically between the curves, cutting right down close to the stitching.

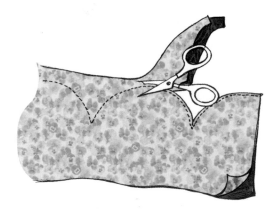

❸ Turn the scalloped edging right side out, ease out the curves using the blunt end of a pencil, and lightly press. Baste the straight edges together.

❹ SEWING THE STRIPED BORDER

Pin a narrow white strip to the right side of a fabric-print strip. Machine stitch ³/₈" from the edge. Press the seam allowance so it lies across the print. Join another white strip to the print in the same way, followed by a strip of the other print and a third white strip.

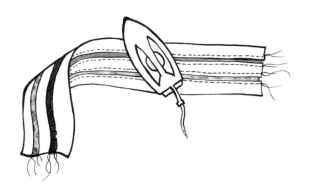

❺ ADDING THE CUFF

Press under ³/₄" along one long edge of the white cuff and lay it out right side up. Place the scalloped edging on top, aligning the raw edges and with the lighter print uppermost. Now place the striped border over the scallops with the darker strip at the top and right side face down. Pin all three layers together along the top edge and machine stitch, leaving a ³/₈" seam allowance. Press the striped border away from the scallops and the cuff.

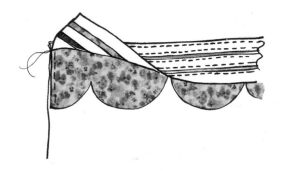

⑥ JOINING ON THE PILLOWCASE

If there is a selvage edge at each end of the darker main pillowcase piece, trim off one of the selvages. With right sides facing, pin the striped border to the raw edge and machine stitch, taking a ³/₈" seam allowance. Press the seam toward the border.

⑦ Fold the folded edge of the cuff over to the wrong side of the pillowcase so that it covers the raw seams. Position the fold so that it overlaps the last seam line by ³/₈", then pin and baste. From the right side, sew the cuff in place by machine stitching along the first white strip, ¹/₈" from the seam line.

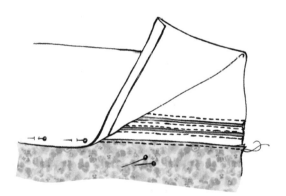

⑧ FINISHING OFF

Measure 27¹/₂" from the top folded edge of the cuff along each raw edge and mark with pins. With right sides together, fold the pillowcase between these pins. Pin the top and bottom edges together starting from the pins and working toward the border.

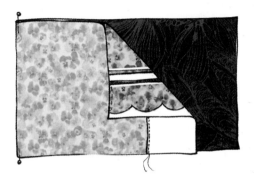

⑨ Turn the remaining flap (with the selvage edge) back over the border and pin the top and bottom edges in place. Machine stitch the top and bottom edges leaving a ⁵/₈" seam allowance. Trim the seams to ¹/₄" and finish with a machine zigzag or overlock stitch. Turn right side out, ease out the corners, and lightly press. Make the second pillowcase in the same way from the remaining pieces of fabric, but positioning the scallop so that the side that contrasts with the main pillowcase will be uppermost on the finished pillowcase.

SEWING TIDY

Great for using up leftovers of furnishing fabric, this portable hanging storage system, with pockets and places for all your sewing notions, means your scissors, needles, and pins are always at hand.

YOU WILL NEED

- 44" x 32" of cream cotton drill fabric
- 52" x 8" of Liberty Linen Union in print of your choice (we used September Roslynd in colorway A)
- 1 yd of matching bias binding
- 8" x 2" of felt
- 8" of narrow lace
- small amount of polyester toy filling
- wooden coat hanger
- sharp pencil
- dressmaker's graph paper
- matching sewing thread
- sewing machine
- sewing kit

TEMPLATES

Copy the templates on page 157, enlarging the pleated pocket template by 400% and all the other templates by 200%.

CUTTING OUT

from cotton drill fabric

front panel	one 19³/₄"-x-23³/₄" rectangle
back panel	one 19³/₄"-x-23³/₄" rectangle
pincushion	one 7³/₄"-x-4" rectangle

from Liberty Linen Union print

pleated pocket
large divided pocket
small divided pocket
large scissor pocket
small scissor pocket
knitting needle pocket

from felt

needlebook cover
needlebook page
strawberry hull

SEPTEMBER ROSLYND *is a hand-drawn Art Nouveau graphic design from a dress fabric for the Liberty autumn/winter 2009 collection.*

❶ SHAPING THE FRONT AND BACK PANELS

Mark the center of a short edge on one panel. Place the coat hanger across this edge with the hook in line with the mark and draw along the upper edge of the hanger. Extend the curve out to the side edges, then neatly cut along the marked line. Use this piece as a template to shape the top of the second panel.

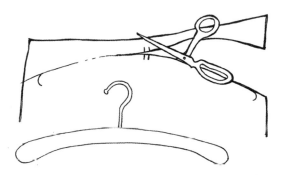

❷ MAKING THE PLEATED POCKET

Press under ½" along the side and bottom edges of the pleated pocket piece, and make a ½" double hem along the top edge by pressing under ½" twice. Insert pins into the top and bottom edges to mark the foldlines, at 1" and 4" intervals, following the broken lines marked on the template. Fold and press each line in turn to create the inverted pleats.

❸

Pin the pleats together and position the pocket centrally on the front panel, 2" up from the bottom edge. Pin and baste the side edges, then machine stitch ⅛" from the fold. Now baste down the bottom edge and stitch through all the layers, ⅛" from the edge. Divide up the pockets by hand stitching a vertical line down the center of each inverted pleat. If you prefer, you can sew this and the other pockets on by hand with small slipstitches.

❹ ADDING THE SMALL POCKETS

Bind the top edge of all five pockets with bias binding (see page 11 for how to do this). Press under ⅜" along the bottom edge of each pocket, then press under ⅜" along the side edges. Fold the corners down and press them too, so that they don't project above the top edge. Press the divided pockets in half and then into quarters to mark the stitching lines.

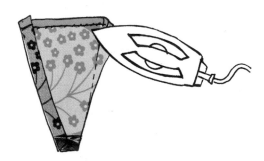

5 Following the photograph as a guide, pin the knitting needle pocket and the large scissor pocket above and to the left of the pleated pocket and the small scissor pocket to the right.

6 Position the divided pockets in the top right half, with the right edges in line with the pleated pocket. Machine stitch in place, 1/8" from the folds, then sew along the crease lines on the divided pockets.

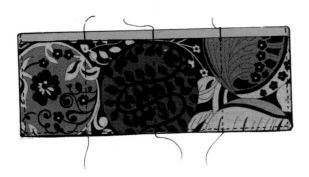

7 SEWING THE STRAWBERRY

With right sides together, join the two straight edges of the strawberry with a 1/4" seam. Trim a small triangle from the tip, then turn right side out. Sew small running stitches around the top edge and stuff firmly with toy filling. Pull up the thread ends to gather and securely fasten off. Cut a 4" length of lace and fold it in half. Sew the ends together and thread on the hull. Stitch the ends of the lace to the top of the strawberry and sew down the tips of the hull.

8 ASSEMBLING THE NEEDLEBOOK

Fold the remaining lace in half and sew the ends to the center top edge of the cover. Pin the felt page to the cover and hand stitch the left edge in place. Fold the book in half and work a few stitches through the spine to keep the book flat. Stitch the top of both lace loops to the front panel.

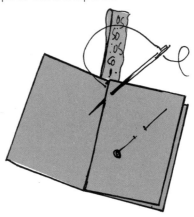

9 PUTTING IT ALL TOGETHER

Pin the front and back panels with right sides together. Machine stitch 5/8" from the edge along the side and top edges, leaving a 3/8" opening at the center top, where marked. Press the seam open, then press under 3/8" along both bottom edges. Turn right side out. Insert the coat hanger, pushing the hook up through the opening. Pin and baste the front to the back along the bottom edge and sew together by hand or machine.

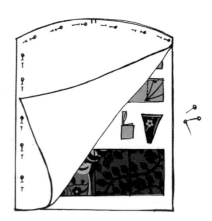

GRAFFITI TABLE RUNNER

This update on the classic table runner combines traditional sewing with unconventional spray paint. The double discs of Liberty Tana Lawn are juxtaposed with vintage doilies colored neon pink.

YOU WILL NEED

- 20"-wide natural linen runner, 12" longer at each end than your table
- 20" x 12" of Liberty Tana Lawn in print of your choice for the main fabric (we used Mauverina in colorway E)
- 26" x 10" of Liberty Tana Lawn in print of your choice for the contrasting fabric (we used Mauvey in colorway B)
- 34" x 14" of pale blue cotton fabric
- 24" x 12" gray cotton fabric
- bright fuchsia sewing thread
- 2¼ yd of 17"-wide iron-on fusible bonding web
- selection of old lace and crochet doilies
- neon pink spray paint
- air-erasable fabric pen or tailor's chalk
- sewing machine
- sewing kit

① STENCILING THE DOILIES

Lay the linen runner out on a flat surface outdoors or in a well-ventilated room. Protect any floor coverings or nearby furniture with newspaper. Place a lace or crochet doily halfway over one end and spray the bottom 3¼" with neon paint, holding the can 8" from the linen and spraying evenly along the hem. Repeat at the other end.

MAUVEY is based on a mixture of mallow shrub flowers and sequins, designed by Liberty's design studio for spring/summer 2008. It has been re-scaled and recolored for the Classic Tana Lawn range.

2 Position three other doilies across the runner, 40" and 20" in from each end and one near the center, close to the side edge. Spray over them in the same way. When the paint is dry, remove the doilies to reveal the beautiful pattern left on the fabric.

3 DRAWING THE FABRIC CIRCLES

The easiest way to make a perfect circle is to draw around a plate or saucer, so sort through your kitchen cupboard to find a good selection of crockery in various sizes. The eight circles used here are 13", 11", 10½", 8¾", 8¼", 7¾", 6¼", and 6" in diameter, but this is a very individual project and each runner will be different.

4 Position all the plates (except the 10½" and 8¾" ones) upside down on the paper side of the fusible bonding web in turn and draw around the outside edge with a pencil. Write the size of the plate on the paper, so you will be able to identify the circles. Leave about ³⁄₈" around each outline.

5 Cut out each bonding web circle roughly and iron them onto the wrong side of the fabrics, following the manufacturer's instructions. Press the 11" and 6" circles to the main print; the 8¼", 7¾", and 6¼" circles to the contrasting print; and the 13" circle to the pale blue cotton. Now cut out each circle accurately around the pencil line.

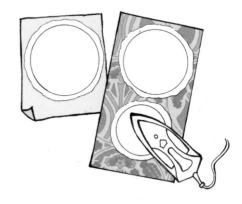

6 MAKING THE DOUBLE-SIDED CIRCLES

The small pale blue and the gray circles that project over the edge of the runner are double-sided. Cut two 10" squares from the remaining pale blue fabric and iron a 10" square of fusible bonding web to the wrong side of one of them. Peel off the backing paper. Draw around the 8¾" plate onto the wrong side of the other square using an air-erasable fabric pen or tailor's chalk. Pin the two squares with right sides together and machine stitch around the line, leaving about 4" unstitched for turning right side out.

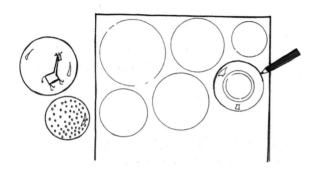

7 Trim away the surplus fabric, leaving a ⅛" seam allowance and cutting straight across the opening. Turn right side out through the opening, ease out the seam, and press. As you press you will activate the fusible bonding web's adhesive and the two sides of the circle will fuse together. Do the same with the gray fabric, cutting it into two 12" squares and drawing around the 10½" plate.

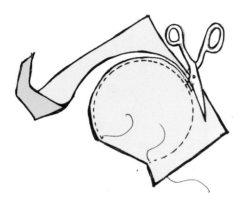

8 ARRANGING THE CIRCLES

Spread the linen runner across your table, making sure there is an equal overhang at each end. Position the double-sided circles so that they project beyond the side edges and arrange the other circles until you have finalized the layout. Be sure to cover up to straight, open edge of each double-sided circle with another overlapping circle. Take a picture for reference.

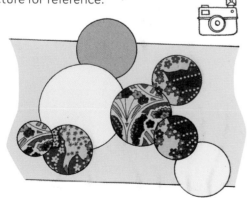

9 Iron the bonding web to the parts of the double-sided circles that will lie over the linen and peel off the backing paper.

10 TRIMMING OFF THE OVERLAPS

To ensure the overlapping layers lie flat you will need to cut away part of each lower circle. To do this, draw around the uppermost circles with an air-erasable fabric pen onto the circles below. Cut away the marked segments from the underlying circles.

11 PRESSING THE CIRCLES IN PLACE

Reposition the circles, overlapping them slightly so that all the raw edges are concealed. Pin down, then transfer the runner to the ironing board. Press down the circles with a hot iron.

12 EMBROIDERING THE EDGES

Thread the machine with bright fuchsia sewing thread and set the controls to a blanket or zigzag stitch. Carefully and slowly stitch around the circumference of each circle.

13 ADDING THE FINISHING TOUCH

Arrange the three now-pink doilies on the runner, pin them in place and stitch in place by hand.

PAJAMA PANTS

*These relaxed pull-on pants are just
perfect for those lazy days at home.
The deep contrasting cuffs can be rolled
up, giving plenty of growing space.*

YOU WILL NEED

- 53" x 28" of Liberty Tana Lawn in print of your choice for the main fabric (we used All Kinds of Families in colorway A for the boy's pants and Nina Taylor in colorway C for the girl's pants)
- 53" x 20" of Liberty Tana Lawn in print of your choice for the contrasting fabric (we used Betsy Ann in colorway B for the boy's pants and Mitsi Valeria in colorway B for the girl's pants)
- ⅝"-wide elastic
- matching sewing thread
- dressmaker's graph paper
- large safety pins
- sewing machine and sewing kit
- sewing kit

TEMPLATES

Select the relevant size from the pattern templates on page 154. Enlarge the pant leg, cuff, and waistband pattern piece outlines onto dressmaker's graph paper (see page 9 for how to do this). Check the size before cutting out the fabric and make any necessary adjustments.

CUTTING OUT

from Liberty Tana Lawn main print
two legs (one reversed)—mark the back of each leg with a safety pin

from Liberty Tana Lawn contrast print
two cuffs
one waistband

FINISHED SIZES

To fit ages	3–4	5–6	7–8	years
To fit waist	15¾"	17¼"	19"	

NINA TAYLOR *is a simple design of hand-painted sandalwood leaves inspired by the fragrance "Avignon" by Comme des Garçons.*

❶ ADDING THE CUFF

Press under ³⁄₈" along the bottom edge of each cuff. With right sides together, pin and baste the top edges of the cuffs to the bottom edges of the pant legs. Machine stitch with a ³⁄₈" seam, then press the seam allowance toward the cuff.

❷ STITCHING THE INSIDE LEG SEAMS

With right sides together, fold the pant legs in half lengthwise. Pin the leg seams together, carefully matching up the points where the cuff seam meets up. Baste, and then machine stitch ³⁄₈" from the edge.

❸ FINISHING THE SEAM EDGES

Press open the seam allowance along the cuff, using the tip of the iron. Trim the rest of the seam allowance to ¼" and finish with a machine zigzag or overlock stitch.

❹ TURNING UP THE CUFF

Fold the cuff in half and pin the pressed-under edge to the pant leg, so that it lies just above the seam line. Baste in place, then turn the legs right side out and machine stitch ⅛" below the top of the cuff. Press lightly.

❺ SEWING THE LEGS TOGETHER

With the right sides together, pin the two pant legs together at the point where the two inside leg seams meet. Pin the seams together at front and back, then machine stitch with a ³⁄₈" seam. Trim the seam allowance to ¼" and finish with a machine zigzag or overlock stitch.

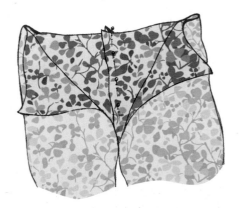

➏ ADDING THE WAISTBAND

Press under ³/₄" along each short end of the waistband and check that it fits snugly around the pajama waist. Press under ³/₈" along the top edge. With right side of waistband and wrong side of pants together and raw edges aligned, pin one end of the waistband to the center front of the waistline. Pin and baste it in place all the way around, then machine stitch with a ³/₈" seam.

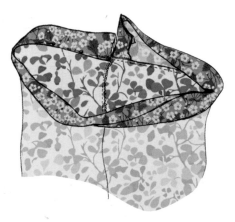

➐ Turn the folded edge over to the right side so that it encloses the raw edges. Pin and baste in place, overlapping the seam line by ¹/₈". Turn right side out and machine topstitch around the waistband, close to the seam.

➑ THREADING THE ELASTIC

Trim one end of the elastic to a sharp point and fasten on a strong safety pin. Mark the final waist measurement on the elastic. Thread the safety pin through the opening at the front of the waistband, and all the way around and back out the other side.

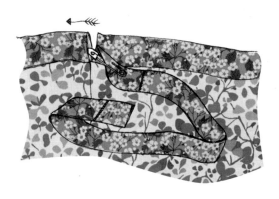

➒ FINISHING OFF THE WAISTBAND

Match up the end of the elastic with the mark made in step 8 and machine stitch very securely through both layers of elastic. Trim off the ends and swivel the elastic around so that the join lies inside the waistband. Slipstitch the opening closed. Make a tiny tab of contrasting fabric and sew it to the inside back edge of the waistband so that the pants will always be worn the right way around.

➓ ADDING A BOW

The girl's version has a small bow. Cut a 10³/₄"-x-2" strip of fabric and fold in half lengthwise with right sides together. Pin together, then machine stitch around the three sides with a ¹/₄" seam allowance, leaving a 1¹/₄" opening in the center of the long edge. Clip the corners and turn right side out by pushing the ends through the opening with a pencil. Push out the corners and press flat. Tie into a bow and sew very securely to the waistband.

PICNIC BAG

This practical tote bag, with an ample number of pockets both inside and out, provides the perfect picnic accessory for summer days spent outdoors.

YOU WILL NEED

- 44" x 40" of heavyweight cream canvas or linen fabric
- 44" x 20" of Liberty Lifestyle craft fabric in print of your choice (we used Copeland in colorway E)
- 44" x 24" of plain cotton fabric in matching color
- 4 yd of 1"-wide heavy woven cotton tape
- 4" x 15" of corrugated plastic, for the base
- 30" x 17" of iron-on fusible bonding web
- double-sided carpet tape
- matching sewing thread
- dressmaker's graph paper
- air-erasable fabric pen
- sewing machine
- sewing kit

TEMPLATE

Copy the template on page 156, enlarging it by 200%, and cut out the outer pocket paper pattern piece.

CUTTING OUT

from canvas or linen fabric
bag pieces   two 21³/4"-x-15³/4" rectangles

from plain cotton fabric
lining   two 21³/4"-x-15³/4" rectangles
pocket bindings   six 10"-x-3¼" strips

from Liberty Lifestyle craft fabric
inner pocket   two 10"-x-8" rectangles

❶ MAKING THE OUTSIDE POCKETS

The stiffened outer pockets are made by fusing together two layers of fabric. Draw around the outer pocket template six times onto the paper side of the bonding web and cut out just outside the outline.

COPELAND *is based on a 1965 design by Friedlande di Colbertaldo Dinzl for Liberty. It was printed at Liberty's Merton Abbey Print Works on silk in 1966.*

❷ Following the manufacturer's instructions, position the shapes, with the paper side upward, on the wrong side of the fabric print. Press them down with a hot iron and then roughly cut out. Peel off the backing papers, press the pockets onto the canvas and cut out along the pencil outlines.

❸ BINDING THE POCKET EDGES

Press under ¼" along one long edge of each binding strip. With right sides together, pin and baste the raw edge of a strip to the top edge of the front of each pocket, centering it. Machine stitch in place, ⅝" from the edge of the binding. Turn the folded edge to the wrong side and slipstitch it in place.

❹ PREPARING THE BAG PIECES

The two bag pieces are prepared in the same way. Draw a 2" square at the bottom corners of both pieces and cut out.

❺ MARKING THE GUIDELINES

Using an air-erasable fabric pen, draw a horizontal line across one bag piece, 3½" from the bottom edge. Mark the center of this line, then mark two points 3¼" and 3½" away from this on each side. Draw two vertical 10" lines up from these points. Mark them 2" from the top for the top edge of the pockets. Add two more vertical lines, ⅜" in from the outside edges.

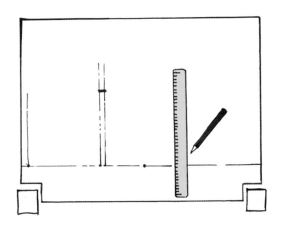

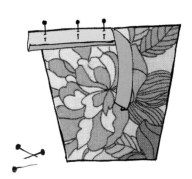

❻ SEWING ON THE POCKETS

Remember to use a thicker machine needle when sewing through the canvas. Line up the center of the bottom edge of the first pocket with the center point on the horizontal line, then pin and baste it in place. Machine stitch with a wide zigzag, reinforcing both ends of the line with a few reverse stitches. Join the side edges along the vertical lines in the same way. The pocket will now project out from the bag. Add one more pocket on each side, following the other lines. Repeat for the second bag piece.

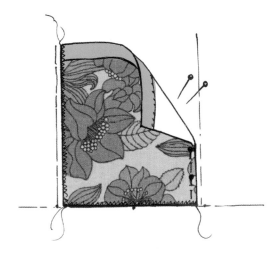

❼ ADDING THE HANDLES

Cut two 40" lengths of cotton tape. Pin the ends of one to each panel between the top of the vertical lines and the bottom edge. Baste, then stitch in place along each edge with matching thread, using a machine blanket stitch or zigzag stitch.

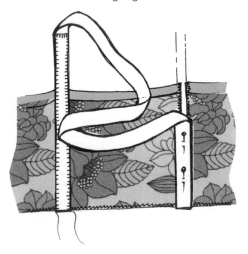

❽ CONCEALING THE RAW EDGES

Cut two 2¹³⁄₄" lengths of cotton tape. Pin and baste one to each bag panel, 3¹⁄₄" up from the bottom edge. Check that the ends line up at the side edges of each bag piece and stitch in place as before.

❾ JOINING THE BAG PIECES

Place the two bag pieces with right sides together. Pin and baste the side and bottom edges, carefully matching the points where the pockets and tape meet. Machine stitch ³⁄₄" from the edge.

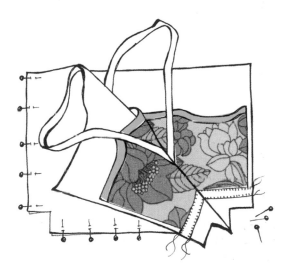

⑩ STITCHING THE CORNERS

Press the seams open from the wrong side, using the tip of the iron so you don't crush the pockets. Refold the open corners at an angle so the side and bottom seams meet in the middle. Pin and baste together, then machine stitch, leaving a $5/8$" seam allowance.

⑪ REINFORCING THE OPENING AND BASE

Press under $5/8$" around the top edge of the bag and sew it down with three rounds of wide zigzag stitch. Press under another $3/4$". Place the plastic rectangle inside the bag to check it fits snugly within the base. Trim if necessary, then secure in place with double-sided carpet tape.

⑫ MAKING THE INNER POCKET

Sew a double $1/4$" hem along the top edge of one inner pocket piece. Pin and baste both pieces with right sides together, matching the side and bottom edges. Machine stitch $3/8$" from the edge, then trim the seam allowance to $1/4$" and finish with a machine zigzag or overlock stitch. Turn the pocket right side out and press.

⑬ ADDING THE LINING

Join the two lining pieces as for the main bag, sewing the side and bottom seams first, then the corners. Press the seams open, but keep it wrong side out. Slip the lining inside the bag, matching the side seams, then pin the top edge around the opening in line with the bottom of the hem. Pin the inner pocket centrally to one side of the bag, $3/8$" down from the top of the lining, and baste through all the layers.

⑭ Fold and baste the top hem of the bag over once again to enclose the raw edges of the lining and stitch it down $1/8$" from the folded edge. Work a final round of stitches $1/8$" down from the top edge.

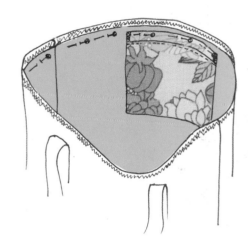

PET BED

—————————— • ——————————

Every dog or cat lover's home houses a pet bed, but often they are difficult to find in attractive fabrics. Making your own from a robust fine corduroy Liberty print solves this décor dilemma.

YOU WILL NEED

• 55" x 67" of Liberty Kingly Cord in print of your choice (we used Jack and Charlie in colorway A)
• 32" x 24" of plain furnishing-weight fabric
• 26½ ounces of safety-standard polyester filling
• matching sewing thread
• sewing machine
• dressmaker's graph paper
• sewing kit

TEMPLATE

Copy the template on page 156, enlarging it by 200%, and cut out the side panel paper pattern piece.

JACK AND CHARLIE *is a conversational pear print inspired by a furnishing design in the Liberty archive originally created in the early 1990s by the Jack Prince Studio.*

✂

CUTTING OUT

from Liberty Kingly Cord print

Make sure that the top edges of the front panel, back panel, and sides all line up on the same part of the pattern repeat.

front panels	two 29½"-x-9¾" rectangles
back panels	two 29½"-x-9¾" rectangles
side panels	four 19¾"-x-9¾" rectangles
inner base	one 29½"-x-19¾" rectangle

from plain furnishing fabric

outer base	one 29½"-x-19¾" rectangle

Prepare the inner and outer bases by marking a ⅝" square at each corner.

NOTE

The seam allowance is ⅝" throughout.

❶ SHAPING THE FRONT PANELS

Draw the full-size front-panel template onto dressmaker's graph paper and cut out. Fold a front-panel fabric rectangle in half widthwise and pin the template through both layers, with the left edge on the fold. Cut along the curved edge. Cut out the other front panel in the same way.

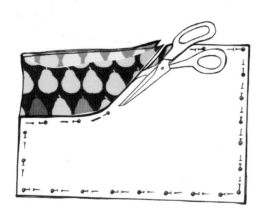

❷ JOINING THE TOP PIECES

With right sides together, pin the ends of two side panels to a back panel. Pin a front panel to the other two ends. Machine stitch, from the top corner downward, leaving the bottom ⅝" unstitched and reinforcing both ends of each seam with a few reverse stitches. Press the seams open. Join the other two side panels to the other back panel and the other front panel in the same way for the inside of the bed.

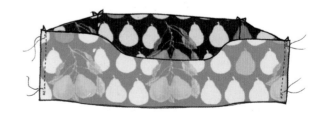

❸ ADDING THE BASE

With right sides together, pin and baste the bottom edge of the outer top to the front, back, and sides of the plain outer base. The pressed-back seam allowances should line up with the edges of the corner squares.

❹ With the top uppermost, machine stitch together with a ⅝" seam, turning the fabric 90 degrees at each corner. Reinforce the stitching at each corner. Press the seam open.

❺ Sew the outer bed together in the same way, but leave a 16" opening in the center of the back seam. Press under the seam allowance on each side of this opening.

❻ JOINING THE INSIDE AND OUTSIDE

Pin the two beds with right sides together, lining up the corner seams. Pin, baste, and machine stitch all the way around the upper edge. Clip into the seam allowance along the curves (see page 13 for how to do this), then turn the bed right side out through the opening at the back.

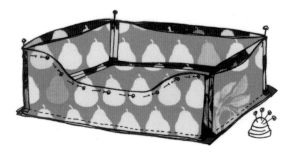

❼ STUFFING THE BED

Using a double length of sewing thread, and small running stitches, sew the two layers together along the four corner seams.

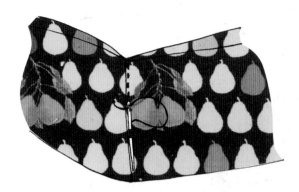

❽ Reaching right inside the cover, stuff the front section with toy filling, distributing it evenly. Close the section by pinning the inside and outside together along the seam line. Hand stitch along this seam line as for the sides. Fill the side and back sections in the same way, then stuff the base. Sew the two sides of the opening securely together to complete.

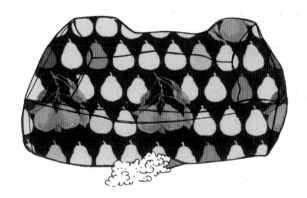

SEWING MACHINE COVER AND BAG

Liven up your sewing machine when it's not in use by making this slip-on dust cover. The additional drawstring bag stores the machine's foot pedal or other sewing effects.

for the sewing machine cover
- 48" x 48" of heavy calico fabric
- 53" x 12" of Liberty Tana Lawn in print of your choice for the main print (we used Manuela in colorway E)
- 53" x 8" of Liberty Tana Lawn in print of your choice for the contrasting print (we used Marco in colorway A)
- 12" x 8" of iron-on fusible bonding web
- sharp pencil
- air-erasable fabric pen or chalk pencil
- matching and contrasting sewing threads
- sewing machine
- sewing kit

for the drawstring bag
- 16" x 26" of Liberty Tana Lawn in print of your choice for the main print (we used Manuela in colorway E)
- 18" x 30" of Liberty Tana Lawn in print of your choice for the contrasting print (we used Marco in colorway A)
- 2¼ yd of ½"-wide ribbon
- four ¾"-diameter wooden beads
- large safety pin

SIZE NOTE
The cover is designed to fit most standard home sewing machines. Copy and enlarge the side panel template on page 155 and check the size against your machine, adjusting if necessary. You may then need to alter the length of the main cover to fit.

TEMPLATES
Copy the templates on page 155, copying the tie end template at 100% and enlarging all the other templates by 200%. Cut out the side panel, pocket, sewing machine motif, and tie end paper pattern pieces.

CUTTING OUT

FOR THE SEWING MACHINE COVER

from calico fabric
main cover	one 17¾"-x-26½" rectangle
lining	one 17¾"-x-27½" rectangle
two side panels	
two pockets	

from Liberty Tana Lawn main print
two side panels

from Liberty Tana Lawn contrasting print
cover edging	two 17¾"-x-1¼" strips
pocket edging	two 10"-x-3¼" strips

FOR THE DRAWSTRING BAG

from Liberty Tana Lawn main print
main bag	one 12½"-x-22¾" rectangle

from Liberty Tana Lawn contrasting print
lining	one 12½"-x-26¾" rectangle
tie ends	four (cut on the fold)

making the sewing machine cover

❶ CUTTING OUT THE APPLIQUÉ SHAPES

Trace the reversed sewing machine, handle, and spool onto the paper side of the fusible bonding web with a sharp pencil and roughly cut out the three shapes. Following the manufacturer's instructions, iron the sewing machine shape onto the wrong side of the main fabric print, and the handle and spool onto the contrasting fabric print.

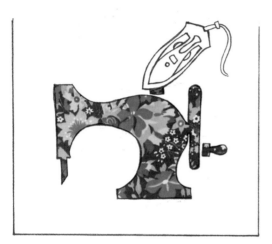

❷ Cut neatly around each outline and peel off the backing papers. Position the sewing machine shape on the main calico cover piece, $2^3/4$" up from the bottom edge. Press in place, then add the handle and spool.

❸ STITCHING AROUND THE SHAPES

Using an air-erasable fabric pen or chalk pencil, draw in the swirling line of thread. Using a narrow satin or blanket stitch, machine stitch around the edge of the sewing machine shape using a thread to match the fabric. Change to a contrasting sewing thread, then stitch around the handle, the spool, and along the thread line.

❹ EDGING THE MAIN CALICO COVER PIECE

With right sides together, pin an edging strip to each short edge of the main calico cover. Baste in place, then machine stitch $3/8$" from the edge. Press the seam allowance toward the print.

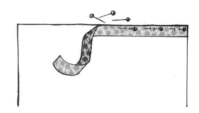

❺ EDGING THE POCKETS

Fold the pocket edging in half lengthwise with the right side facing outward. Pin the folded strip centrally to the wrong side of the pocket, along the top edge, aligning the raw edges. Machine stitch, leaving a seam allowance of $3/8$", then turn the edging over to the right side and press. Trim the ends in line with the side edges of the pocket.

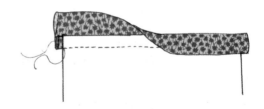

❻ BASTING ON THE POCKETS

Fold the side panel in half lengthwise and mark the center top. Pin and baste the prepared pocket to the panel, aligning the side and bottom edges.

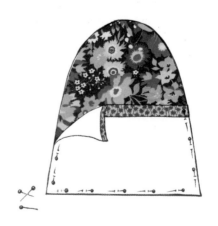

❼ ASSEMBLING THE MAIN-COVER PIECES

Fold the cover in half widthwise and mark the center of each side edge. With right sides together, pin on one of the side panels, matching up the center points and the corners. Baste the two together close to the edge and machine stitch, leaving a ¼" seam allowance. Add the second side panel in the same way. Turn right side out and press lightly.

❽ ASSEMBLING THE LINING

Make the calico lining in the same way, but omitting the edging and leaving a 6" opening in the seam line along the side edge of one side panel. Press under the seam allowance on both sides of the opening.

❾ SEWING THE LINING TO THE COVER

With right sides together, slip the lining inside the main cover. Matching up the four seams, pin the two bottom edges together. Baste and machine stitch ⅜" from the edge. Turn right side out through the opening, then slipstitch the opening closed. Now push the lining back inside the cover. Press the bottom edge so the seam line sits along the fold. Machine stitch along the seam line along the top of the edging to stabilize the hem.

making the drawstring bag

❶ ASSEMBLING THE MAIN BAG

Fold the main bag piece in half widthwise with right sides together. Pin and baste the side edges, then machine stitch with a ⅜" seam. Now clip a small triangle from each bottom corner and press the seam allowances inward. Turn the bag right side out.

❷ PREPARING THE DRAWSTRING CHANNEL

With the wrong side of the fabric face up, press ¾" to the wrong side along each short edge of the lining piece, then fold 1¼" to the wrong side and press. Unfold both creases.

❸ ASSEMBLING THE LINING

Fold the lining in half widthwise with sides together. Pin and baste, then machine stitch the side edges with a ³⁄₈" seam, leaving a ³⁄₄" opening in each side seam, centrally positioned between the two foldlines. This will be the opening for the ribbons.

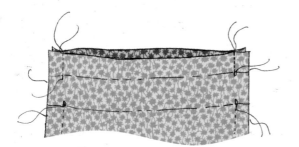

❹ Clip a small triangle from the bottom corners, then press the seam allowances inward as for the main bag. Hand stitch the seam allowance in place along each side of the opening. Refold and re-press the double hem at the top of the lining.

❺ JOINING THE BAG AND LINING

With the bag right side out and the lining wrong side out, slip the lining inside the bag and push it right down into the bottom corners. Fold the double hem over the top edge of the main bag, matching up the side seams. Pin and baste. Using matching thread, machine stitch twice around the hem, ¹⁄₄" from the top edge, then ¹⁄₄" from the bottom edge.

❻ THREADING THROUGH THE TIES

Cut the ribbon in half. Attach a safety pin to one end of the first ribbon and feed it through one of the openings. Push it all the way around the channel and back out. Thread the second ribbon through the other opening in the same way.

❼ ADDING THE BEADS

Trim the ends of the ribbon into narrow points and thread a bead onto each one. Push the beads halfway up the ribbons and cut off the points.

❽ MAKING THE TIE ENDS

Press the tie ends in half widthwise with right sides together. Turn under and press both top edges along the foldline. Baste the side edges and machine stitch with a ¹⁄₄" seam. Clip the corners and turn right side out, using a pencil to ease out the corners.

❾ Push the ends of the ribbons into the tie ends. Baste them in place, then machine stitch close to the top edge. Slide the beads back down the ribbons: the ties ends will gather slightly.

UPHOLSTERED FOOTSTOOL

The flat, smooth surface of a footstool is the perfect canvas for showcasing a favorite print. Why not reclaim an old stool and update the woodwork with a bright shade of paint.

YOU WILL NEED

- Liberty Linen Union in print of your choice (we used Sydenham Hall in colorway A)—see right to calculate the amount of fabric needed
- polyester batting, ¾" smaller all around than the fabric
- block of upholstery foam cut to size, if needed
- matching sewing thread
- double-sided carpet tape
- upholsterer's tacks
- small hammer
- air-erasable fabric pen or chalk pencil
- long ruler
- sewing machine
- sewing kit
- medium-grain sandpaper
- turpentine
- spray primer and paint, or paintbrush, wood primer, and wood paint
- clear varnish

MEASURING YOUR FOOTSTOOL

Measure the width (A), depth (B), and height (C) of the foam block, and the height of the footstool base (D). Use these figures to calculate the size of the batting and fabric.

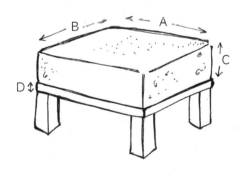

CUTTING OUT

from polyester batting
one rectangle   width = A + 2C
                    depth = B + 2C
                    cut one square ¾" less than than C from each corner

from Liberty Linen Union print
one rectangle   width = A + 2C + 2D + 1½"
                    depth = B + 2C + 2D + 1½"

❶ RENOVATING THE FOOTSTOOL BASE

Remove the existing fabric and tacks. If the original foam is still in good condition, leave it in place and replace the fabric cover to protect it from any stray paint. Sand the frame and legs with medium-grain sandpaper.

❷ Remove any dust and dirt with turpentine and apply the appropriate primer. Finish with two coats of wood paint or four light coats of spray paint, taking care to cover every bit of wood. For a more protected finish, paint with clear varnish. Leave to dry. If you are using new foam, fix it to the top of the stool with double-sided carpet tape.

❸ Lay the batting over the foam and trim the bottom edges in line with the top of the stool. This extra layer will give a smooth look to the cover.

❹ MARKING THE GUIDELINES ON THE FABRIC

Lay the fabric out with the right side face down and, using an air-erasable fabric pen (or chalk pencil) and a long ruler, mark the guidelines. First, draw a line ³⁄₄" in from each side edge, then four lines parallel to these, which lie the same as the height of the foam (measurement C) farther in.

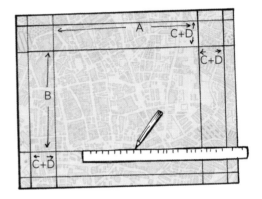

❺ JOINING THE CORNERS

Press under ³⁄₄" around the outside edge, then unfold. Fold the cover so that the right-hand edge lies along the bottom edge, with right sides together. Pin the corner edges (C + D) together, matching up the guidelines. Join the other corners in the same way, then slip the cover over the stool.

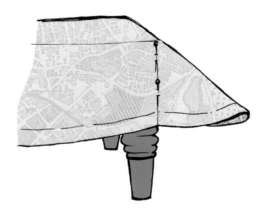

⑥ SEWING THE CORNER SEAMS

Adjust the pins if necessary to get a perfect fit, then baste the seams in line with the pins. Machine stitch from the outside edge inward, to within 1/4" of the point where the guidelines meet. Adjust the angle so the final few stitches slope slightly toward the center of the cover and continue to the end. This will give a neatly rounded look to the corners.

⑦ PRESSING THE SEAMS AND HEMMING

Trim away the excess fabric at the corners, leaving a 3/8" seam allowance and tapering it to 1/8" at the top. Press the four seams open. Turn under and re-press the bottom hem, then baste it in place. (If you wish, you can baste contrasting braid over the hem as a background for the tacks.)

⑧ MARKING THE TACK POSITIONS

Make a series of pencil or chalk marks around the top edge of the footstool so the tacks will be regularly spaced. Start by marking the midpoint of each side, then a point 3/8" in from each corner. Divide the rest of the length at 1 1/4"–1 1/2" intervals.

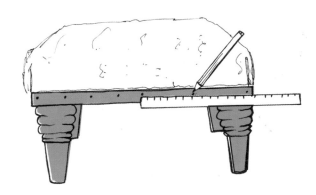

⑨ ATTACHING THE COVER

Starting at one midpoint, gently pull the fabric down until the edge is level with the bottom edge of the footstool top. Insert an upholsterer's tack through the hem so the rim of the tack touches the edge of the fabric. Hammer it in, at right angles to the stool. Repeat on the opposite side, then the other twosides. Hammer in the corner tacks, then add therest, working from the center outward. Always repeat on one side what you do on the other to maintain the fabric at an even tension across the top of the footstool.

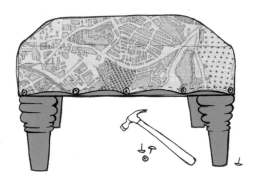

STRIPED
THROW

The beauty of this quilt is its random, spontaneous juxtaposition of fabrics, made easy by the fact that so many Liberty Tana Lawn prints work effortlessly together.

YOU WILL NEED

- I yd of 53"-wide Liberty Tana Lawn in classic print of your choice for the main print (we used Wiltshire in colorway R)
- ²/₃ yd of 53"-wide Liberty Tana Lawn in each of five more prints (we used Felix and Isabelle in colorway B; Kayoko in colorway D; Mabelle in colorway C; Mark Gosling in colorway C; and Small Susanna in colorway D)
- 61" square of cotton quilt batting
- matching sewing thread
- quilting thread
- sewing machine
- sewing kit
- one or two thimbles
- quilter's safety pins

FINISHED SIZE
The finished throw measures approximately 57½" square.

CUTTING OUT

from Liberty Tana Lawn main print
Join two pieces to achieve the required length for the side borders and the binding.

top border	one 4" x 51" strip
bottom border	one 4" x 51" strip
side borders	two 4" x 57½" strips
binding	four 2" x 59" strips

❶ MAKING THE CENTER PANEL

The center panel is made up of randomly arranged stripes, each one a narrow strip of a fabric print between 2" and 3¼" wide. The quickest way to prepare these is to make a small snip into the selvage, tear across the full width of the fabric, and press well to flatten out the edges. Pin two strips together lengthwise with right sides together and machine stitch, leaving a ³/₈" seam allowance.

② Press the seam to one side. Continue adding more strips, alternating the fabrics, until the panel is 51" deep. While adding the strips, line them all up on the left-hand side and press all the seam allowances in the same direction. To trim the right edge so that it is perfectly straight, measure a point 51" along the top and bottom edges and draw a line between them. Cut along this line to create a perfect 51" square.

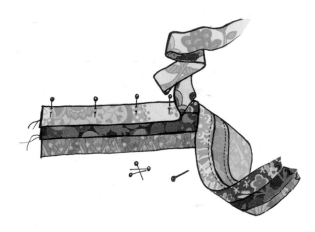

③ ADDING THE BORDERS

Sew the top and bottom borders to the finished center panel with a ³/₈" seam and press the seams outward. Add the two side borders, again pressing the seams outward, and trim the ends as necessary.

④ MAKING THE BACKING

Sew the backing together in the same way, using 4"-wide to 8"-wide strips of the remaining fabric to make a rectangle 51" wide by 63" long. Press the seams open. Make two 6³/₄"-x-63" strips and sew one to each side edge with a ³/₈" seam, for a 63"-square backing.

⑤ ASSEMBLING THE LAYERS

Spread out the backing, right side down, and place the batting centrally on top. Lay the quilt top centrally over the batting, with the right side facing upward. Smooth out the sandwiched layers and, working across from one edge, safety pin them together at 4" intervals.

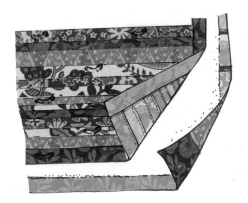

⑥ HAND QUILTING THE SEAMS

The ridged look is created by quilting "in the ditch" or directly on top of the seam lines between the strips. Using quilting thread, sew a line of ¹/₄" running stitches along each seam on the quilt top, preferably using one or two thimbles to protect your fingers.

7 When the quilting is complete, baste around the outside edge of the quilt top to hold the three layers together. Cut off the surplus batting and backing fabric so these layers align with the quilt top.

8 BINDING THE TOP AND BOTTOM EDGES

Press under ³/₈" along one long edge of each binding strip. With right sides together, pin the unfolded edge of the first strip centrally to the top edge of the quilt top, aligning the raw edges and leaving an overlap at each end.

9 Machine stitch ³/₈" from the edge, then turn the binding to the back to enclose the raw edges. Pin down the folded edge, trim the ends in line with the sides of the quilt, and slipstitch the fold to the quilt back. Bind the bottom edge in the same way.

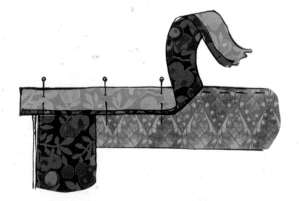

10 BINDING THE SIDE EDGES

Press under ³/₈" at one end of both remaining binding strips. Line the folded end up with the finished edge of the quilt and pin the strip to the quilt as for the top and bottom edges. Trim the other end so that it is ³/₈" longer than the quilt and fold under this overlap.

11 Sew the strip in place and turn the folded edge over to the wrong side. Slipstitch the fold to the quilt back.

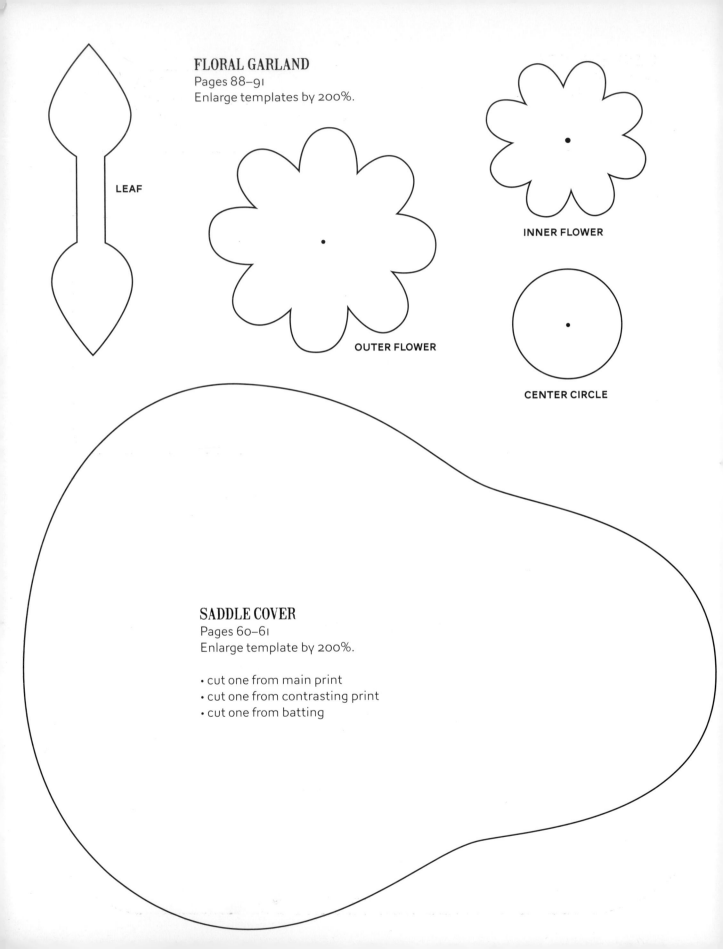

FLORAL GARLAND
Pages 88–91
Enlarge templates by 200%.

LEAF

OUTER FLOWER

INNER FLOWER

CENTER CIRCLE

SADDLE COVER
Pages 60–61
Enlarge template by 200%.

• cut one from main print
• cut one from contrasting print
• cut one from batting

CAFETIERE COVER
Pages 62–65
Enlarge templates by 200%.

TAB
cut one from paper

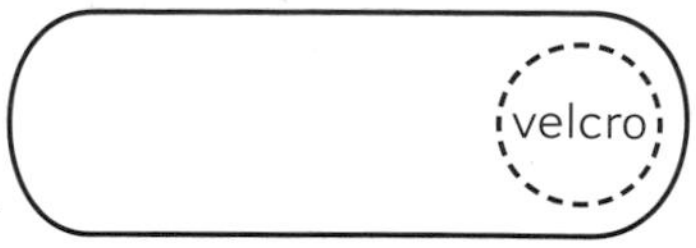

velcro

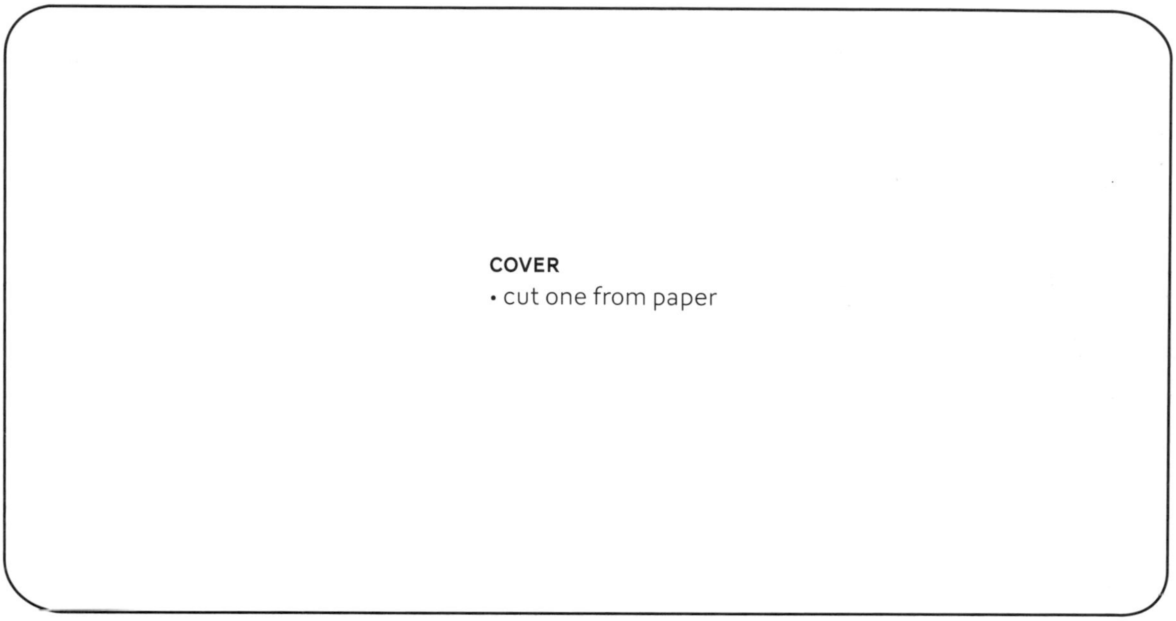

COVER
• cut one from paper

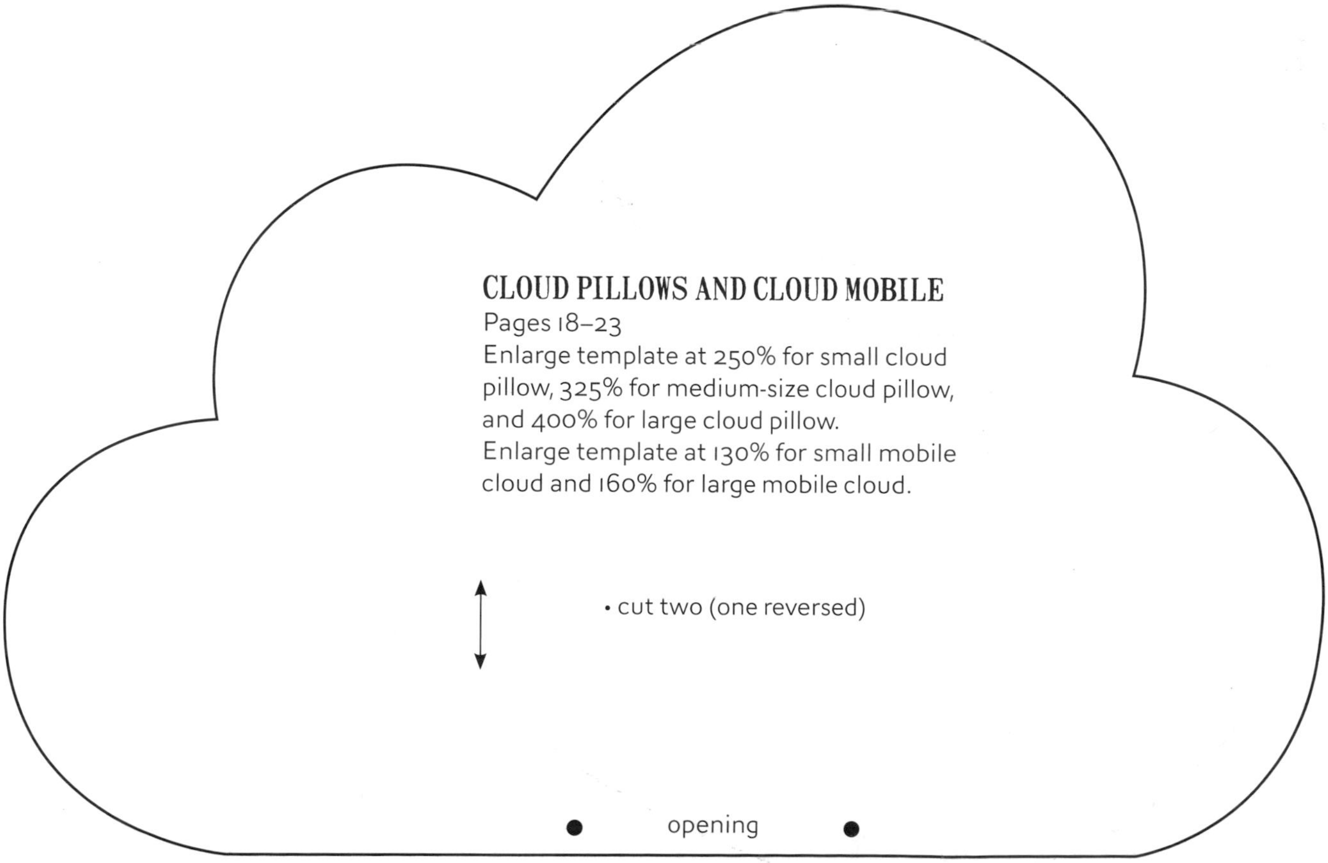

CLOUD PILLOWS AND CLOUD MOBILE
Pages 18–23
Enlarge template at 250% for small cloud pillow, 325% for medium-size cloud pillow, and 400% for large cloud pillow.
Enlarge template at 130% for small mobile cloud and 160% for large mobile cloud.

• cut two (one reversed)

opening

'LIBBY' DOLL

Pages 80–87

Enlarge templates by 200%.

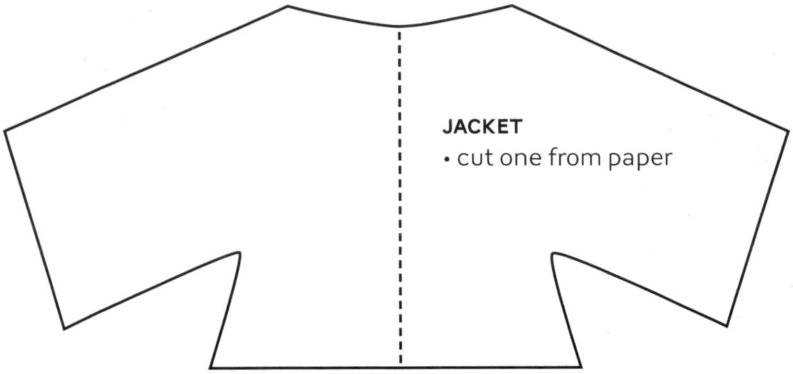

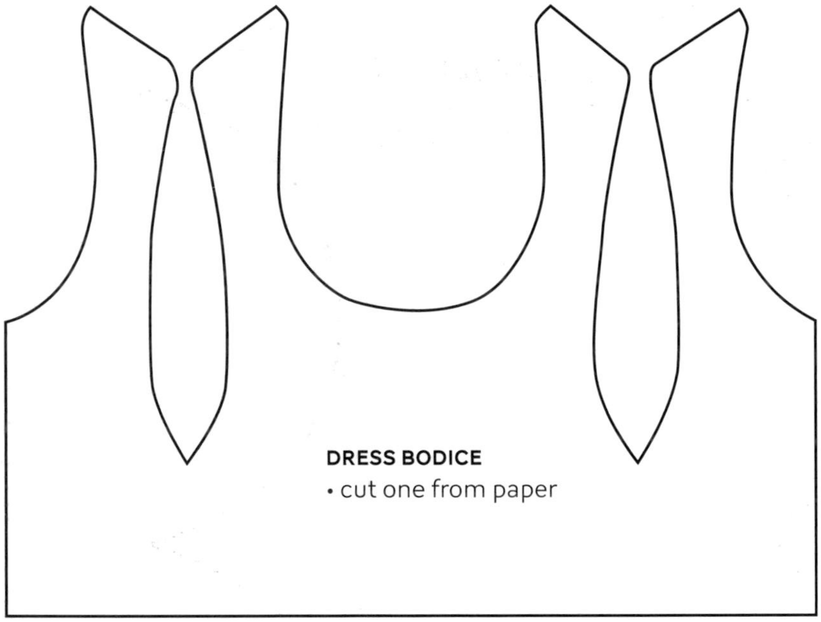

JACKET
· cut one from paper

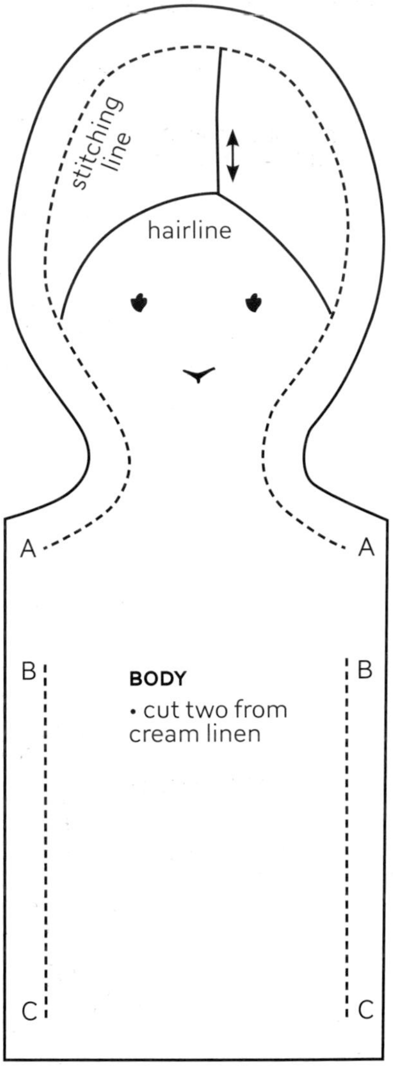

stitching line

hairline

A — — A

B ⋮ **BODY**
· cut two from
cream linen
B

C ⋮ C

DRESS BODICE
· cut one from paper

fold

SHOE
· cut one from paper

ARM
· cut two on fold

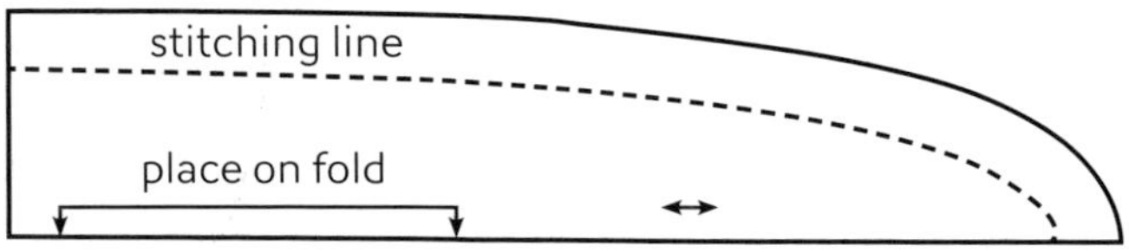

stitching line

place on fold

LEG
· cut two on fold

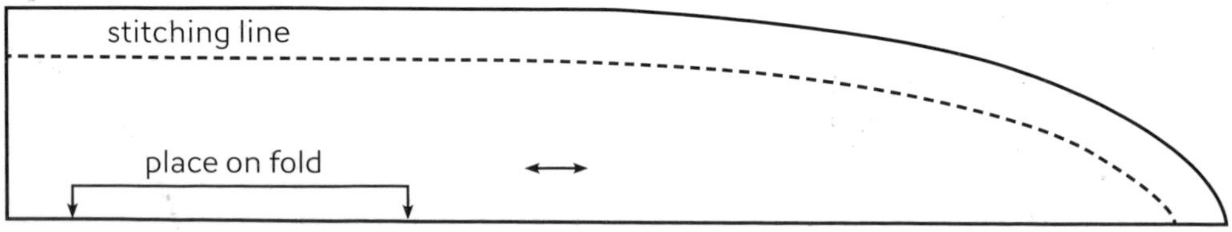

stitching line

place on fold

LEAF PILLOWS
Pages 96–101
Enlarge templates by 400%.

**APPLIQUÉ LEAVES
FOR SMALL PILLOW**

EDGED PILLOWCASES
Pages 102–107
Enlarge template by 200%.

**APPLIQUÉ LEAVES
FOR LARGE PILLOW**

PYJAMA TROUSERS

Pages 118–123
Enlarge templates by 400%.
1 square = ³⁄₄″

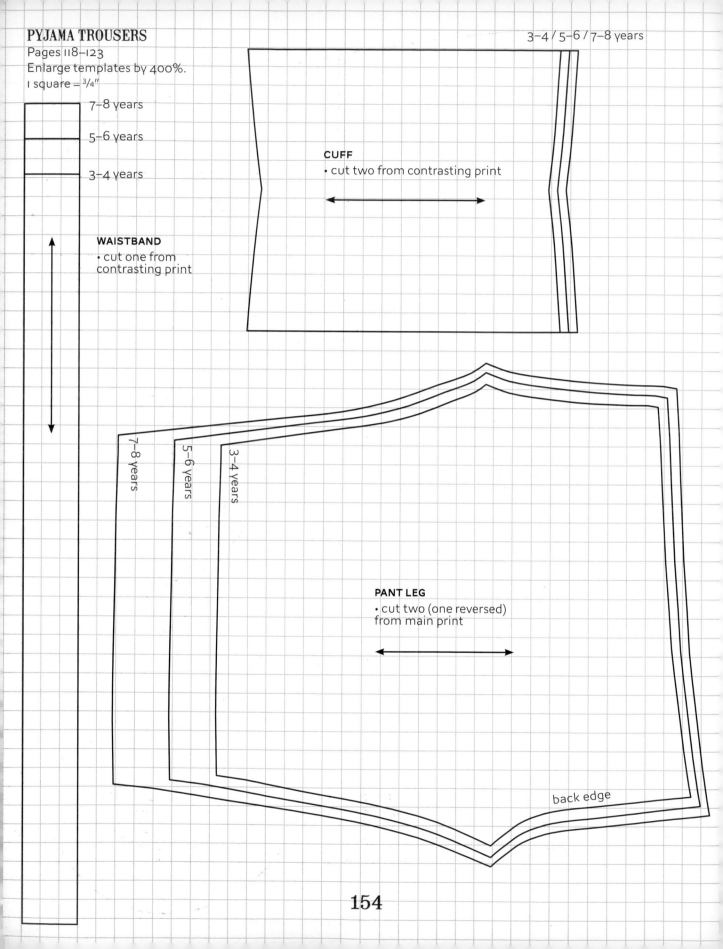

7–8 years

5–6 years

3–4 years

WAISTBAND
• cut one from
contrasting print

CUFF
• cut two from contrasting print

7–8 years

5–6 years

3–4 years

PANT LEG
• cut two (one reversed)
from main print

back edge

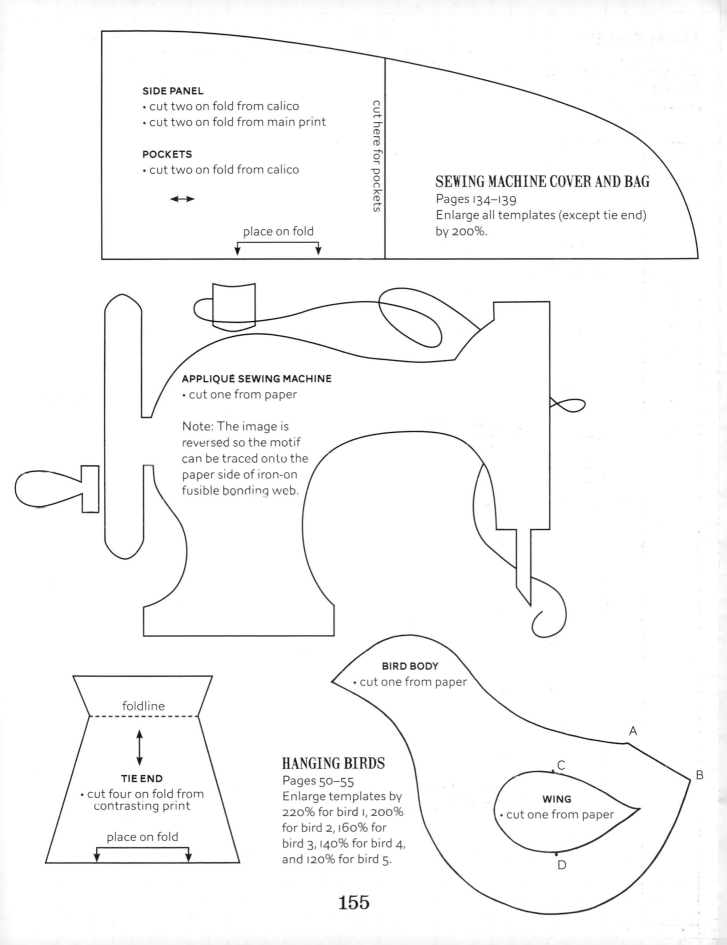

SIDE PANEL
• cut two on fold from calico
• cut two on fold from main print

POCKETS
• cut two on fold from calico

place on fold

cut here for pockets

SEWING MACHINE COVER AND BAG
Pages 134–139
Enlarge all templates (except tie end)
by 200%.

APPLIQUÉ SEWING MACHINE
• cut one from paper

Note: The image is reversed so the motif can be traced onto the paper side of iron-on fusible bonding web.

foldline

TIE END
• cut four on fold from contrasting print

place on fold

HANGING BIRDS
Pages 50–55
Enlarge templates by 220% for bird 1, 200% for bird 2, 160% for bird 3, 140% for bird 4, and 120% for bird 5.

BIRD BODY
• cut one from paper

A

C

B

WING
• cut one from paper

D

OUTER POCKET
• cut one from paper

PICNIC BAG
Pages 124–129
Enlarge template by 200%.

PET BED
Pages 130–133
Enlarge template by 200%.

FRONT PANEL
• cut two on fold from main print

place on fold

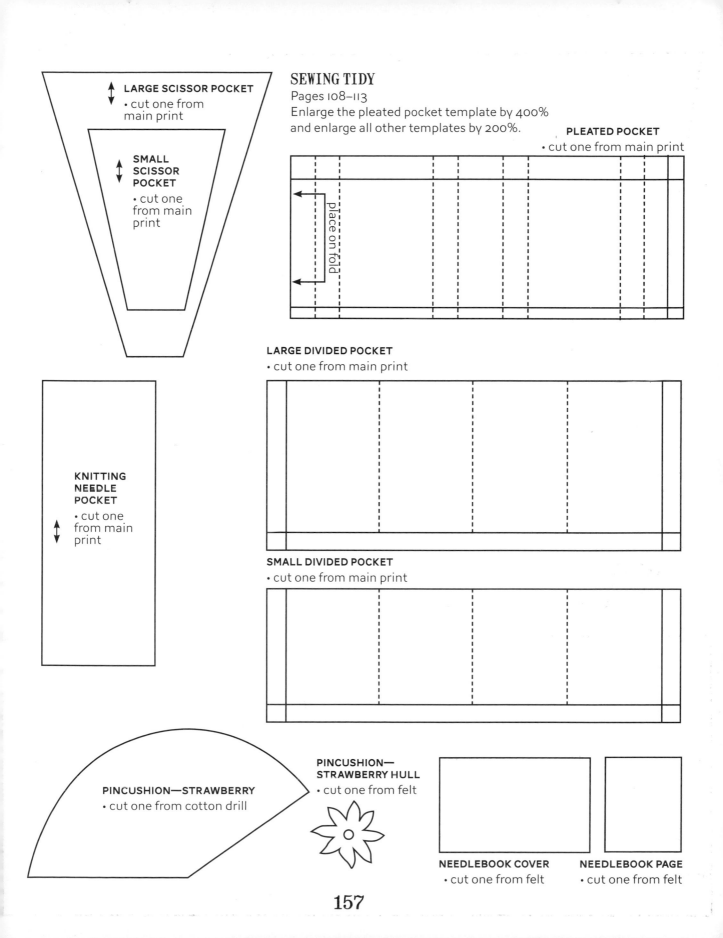

LARGE SCISSOR POCKET
• cut one from main print

SMALL SCISSOR POCKET
• cut one from main print

SEWING TIDY

Pages 108–113
Enlarge the pleated pocket template by 400%
and enlarge all other templates by 200%.

PLEATED POCKET
• cut one from main print

place on fold

LARGE DIVIDED POCKET
• cut one from main print

KNITTING NEEDLE POCKET
• cut one from main print

SMALL DIVIDED POCKET
• cut one from main print

PINCUSHION—STRAWBERRY
• cut one from cotton drill

PINCUSHION— STRAWBERRY HULL
• cut one from felt

NEEDLEBOOK COVER
• cut one from felt

NEEDLEBOOK PAGE
• cut one from felt

157

LIBERTY LIFESTYLE CRAFT FABRIC (44"-wide quilting-weight cotton)

BELL is based on a 1963 Liberty design. It was printed at Liberty's Merton Abbey Print Works on varuna wool.

CATHERINE is based on a 1969 design. It was printed at Liberty's Merton Abbey Print Works on varuna wool in 1971.

COPELAND is based on a 1965 design by Friedlande di Colbertaldo Dinzl for Liberty. It was printed at Liberty's Merton Abbey Print Works on silk in 1966.

CRANSTON is based on an early 1900s artwork found in the Liberty archive.

DANCE is based on a 1991 design by the Jack Prince Studio. It was used in the spring/summer collection of 1993.

GARNETT is based on several 1930s Liberty designs. It was printed at Liberty's Merton Abbey Print Works on wool in 1971.

HERBERT is based on a Liberty design from the early 1900s, when Liberty was renowned for its iconic Art Nouveau designs.

LEONARD was designed by Sholto Drumlanrig, who put together the Liberty Lifestyle craft fabric collection.

LOWKE is based on a Liberty furnishing cretonne from the late 1890s.

MACKINTOSH is inspired by the early 1900s Glasgow School artists and was designed by Sholto Drumlanrig.

NEWBURY is based on a 1965 design by Agnes Roberts for Liberty. It was printed at Liberty's Merton Abbey Print Works on cotton in 1966.

RENNIE is based on a Liberty furnishing linen from the early 1900s.

WOOLF is based on a 1977 design by Allan Thomas for Liberty. It was used in the spring/summer collection of 1979.

LIBERTY KINGLY CORD (a fine corduroy)

JACK AND CHARLIE is a conversational pear print inspired by a furnishing design in the Liberty archive, originally created in the early 1990s by the Jack Prince Studio.

LIBERTY MADAURI COTTON (quilting-weight cotton)

INDIRA is based on a printed gauze design from the late nineteenth century found in the Liberty archive.

PRIYA is based on a bold one-color pattern that was designed especially for the Liberty spring/summer collection of 2007.

TEHZEEB is based on an indigo printed cotton sample from an early 1900s Liberty pattern book.

ZAI is based on a 1995 design by Michael Fieldsend for Liberty, which was used in the spring/summer collection of 1998.

LIBERTY FURNISHING COLLECTION

FELIX RAISON (a Liberty cotton velvet) was inspired by a Liberty dress fabric design that was based on an 1850s paisley shawl drawing found in the Liberty archive.

HEBE (a Liberty Linen Union) is a one-color version of Liberty's famous peacock feather pattern. It has been in the range since the 1890s and is a key print associated with Liberty.

SEPTEMBER ROSLYND (a Liberty Linen Union) is a hand-drawn Art Nouveau graphic design from a dress fabric for the autumn/winter collection of 2009.

SYDENHAM HALL (a Liberty Linen Union) is based on old maps of Crystal Palace, designed for a spring/summer 2004 dress fabric.

LIBERTY TANA LAWN (53"-wide cotton lawn)

ALL KINDS OF FAMILIES is taken from the fingerprints of all the designers in the Liberty Design Studio. The pattern was hand painted and then colored to create an all-over tonal texture.

ARANOV is a graphic hand-drawn lady-and-bird design inspired by the romance of the Secession movement.

BETSY ANN is a miniature version of the famous Liberty classic print "Betsy," which originated in 1933.

FARHAD was inspired by Art Nouveau repeats and mazes of stately gardens in Vienna. The design captures motifs from both art and nature.

FELIX AND ISABELLE was based on a drawing of a paisley shawl from the 1850s found in the Liberty archive.

GLENJADE was created from a 1930s Liberty cotton design. The designer is unknown but the print has been in the Classic Tana collection since 1979.

HUGO GRENVILLE is named after the very established botanical painter. This design is based upon his paintings from the Tresco Abbey Garden in the Isles of Scilly.

JOLIE ROSE was created from the drawings and paintings of five-year-olds at a Parisian primary school. The repeat was inspired by the Breton stripe.

KATIE AND MILLIE is a small floral trail inspired by a design from the Liberty archive originally created in the 1920s.

KAYOKO is an archival floral design from the Liberty Art Fabrics spring/summer collection of 2011.

LODDEN is an original William Morris design, first produced by Morris & Co. in 1884.

MABELLE is inspired by Indian chintz designs of the seventeenth and eighteenth centuries. It was created by the Liberty Design studio especially for the Classic Tana collection in 2007.

MANUELA was inspired by a scarf design from the Liberty archive created in the 1970s. During this period many of Liberty's patterns were based on Liberty's 1930s floral designs.

MARC GOSLING is a geometric leaf design inspired by a rare type of heliconia.

MARCO was a print of tiny trees that was retraced from the original and printed on tints and deep-dyed grounds to create solid blocks of color.

MARINA SEAFLOWER is hand painted from the lush and exotic flora found in the Tresco Abbey Garden in the Isles of Scilly.

MAUVERINA is a modern Art Nouveau floral created by the Liberty Design Studio for the autumn/winter collection 2007.

MAUVEY is a mixture of mallow flowers and sequins, created by Liberty's Design Studio for the spring/summer collection of 2008. It was rescaled for the Classic Tana range in 2011.

MAY ROSE was hand drawn from sunflowers to represent the annual worldwide sunflower planting by the Guerrilla Gardeners on May 1st.

MITSI is based on a design created by Liberty during the 1950s. It plays on Liberty's history with Japanese-style cherry blossom and was in the Liberty Art Fabrics autumn/winter collection of 2008 before becoming a Classic Tana Lawn.

MITSI VALERIA is based on a 1950s design by Gillian Farr. It references Liberty's history with Japanese-style cherry blossom designs.

NINA TAYLOR is a simple design of hand-painted sandalwood leaves inspired by the fragrance "Avignon" by Comme des Garçons.

OCEANID is an original Liberty sketch created in the late 1980s, showing botanicals mixed with vintage objects.

OTTILIA is a fantastical forest design created from digitally manipulating photographs to capture Tresco Abbey Garden's diverse tropical foliage.

PINKY was painted by five-year-olds from St. Bartholomew's School, London.

POINTILLISM was designed using layers of thick oil paint to create a multicolored texture that resembles the wildflower fields of the Tresco Abbey Garden in the Isles of Scilly.

SAEED is an eclectic mixture of hand-drawn photorealistic pansies drawn by Michael Angove and abstract violas by a student of Central Saint Martins College, London.

SCILLY FLORA is a tropical multicolored design that was inspired by the wonderful flora of the Tresco Abbey Garden in the Isles of Scilly.

SMALL SUSANNA was designed by the Liberty Design Studio for the spring/summer collection of 2005. It was then re-scaled and recolored for the Classic Tana range in 2010.

SPECKLE is based on the flowers photographed at the Chelsea Flower Show in London, selected because of their speckled petals for the spring/summer collection of 2013.

TRAVELLING THREADS is a thread drawing designed by Debbie Smyth based on London Transport, created by stretching a network of threads between accurately plotted pins.

TRESCO is a watercolor study of a selection of flowers, ferns, and succulents from the Tresco Abbey Garden in the Isles of Scilly.

WILTSHIRE is a leaf and berry pattern, which was designed for Liberty in 1933. Wiltshire has been in the Classic Tana range since 1979.

XANTHE SUNBEAM depicts scattered golden flora from the Tresco Abbey Garden in the Isles of Scilly, drawn and painted with ink in situ.

LIBERTY
Great Marlborough Street
London W1B 5AH
www.liberty.co.uk

Liberty fabrics are available to buy both instore and online.

PUBLISHER'S ACKNOWLEDGMENTS
Thank you to Liberty for the props supplied throughout the book.

Thank you to Beg Bicycles for the loan of the bicycle on pages 57 & 60.
www.begbicycles.com